The Complete Guide to

Home Picture Framing

Featuring Logan Graphic Equipment and Tools

by Malcolm David Logan

The Complete Guide to Home Picture Framing
by Malcolm David Logan
©2011 Logan Graphic Products, Inc., Wauconda, Illinois

All International Rights Reserved
Second Edition
Printed in the United States of America

ISBN 0-9749683-0-7

Please request permission or further information from Logan Graphic Products, Inc., 1100 Brown Street, Wauconda, IL 60084. Phone 847-526-5515, fax 847-526-5155, info@logangraphic.com

The information in this book is offered in good faith, but without guarantee, because the techniques of individuals and variations in products are beyond our control. We recommend the user determine, for his/her own purposes, the suitability of all materials, methods, and information mentioned. Logan Graphic Products, Inc. and Malcolm David Logan, individually and combined, disclaim all responsibility for loss or damage resulting from the use of the information furnished herein.

Table of Contents

Introduction

The world of picture framing is changing. Time was if you wanted to frame a picture you were obliged to use a professional. The equipment and materials necessary were the exclusive domain of wholesalers who would only sell to those willing to invest the time and capital to start a picture framing business—and that business was defined as a storefront outfitted with fixtures, encumbered with legal and financial obligations, and saddled with a substantial investment in equipment and materials. For those who wanted to start a small framing business from their home, catering to friends and neighbors with the potential for growth—or for the artist or photographer who needed to frame in a professional manner—or for business people who wanted to add picture framing to an existing business—there was no way in.

In 1974 Logan Graphic Products quietly led a revolution. They designed a low-priced mat cutter designed for artists, photographers, and what the industry referred to then with some disdain as "garage framers". The Simplex Mat Cutter took the heft out of a professional frame shop's mat cutter, creating a machine designed to cut an average of 15-25 mats a week, yet retaining all the key ease-of-use features available on professional mat cutters, and at a price the average do-it-yourselfer could afford. The Simplex quickly became Logan's flagship product and grew into a full line of mat cutting equipment with products affordable for any budget.

A common complaint of late has been the cost of picture framing. For those who frame with some regularity, the cost of going to a frame shop is an uncomfortable burden. For those who frame only occasionally, it's a shock! The cost of professional picture framing has climbed in recent years as suppliers and mass merchandisers have shifted the emphasis to costly, archival framing—the Cadillac of framing treatments—and the small, independent frame shops, once the purveyors of a low-priced alternative, have fallen by the wayside. The result has been a professional framing industry devoted almost exclusively to high-end framing. For the man on the street, it seemed there was just no way to frame inexpensively any more.

In basement workshops and on kitchen tables across America a small cadre of devoted craftspeople knew better. With a reasonably priced mat cutter and some store-bought picture frames, they could mat and frame themselves for 50 percent less than the cost of going to a frame shop, and if there was a woodworker in the home, something remarkable could happen. By cutting and joining their own frames, these same craftspeople could take as much as 75 percent out of the cost of traditional framing.

At the other end of the market, traditional picture framing suppliers viewed the stirrings from below as a threat to their livelihood. Consequently, if a home picture framer contacted his local wholesaler looking to purchase picture frame mouldings in length so that he could cut and join his own frames, he was gently but firmly turned away. If he wanted to buy cutting and joining equipment, he was presented with prices that staggered him. And if he wanted to learn how to do it, he was informed that he would need to make a substantial investment in a serious business enterprise and show a financial commitment to his future as a professional picture framer.

It is a credit to those early home framers that against all odds they continued to strive to do their own picture framing. Without easy

Art Courtesy of D.M. Moore

access to equipment or materials, they kept at it, producing quality work. It is a credit to those small business owners who saw picture framing as a viable complementary offering to their main line of business, that they made it happen. It is a credit to artists and photographers everywhere who

refused to hand over a substantial part of their profits for framing that they elected to do it themselves. Given the climate in which they were working, it's a credit to anyone who has done their own picture framing that they have succeeded. And it is due to their determined efforts that the world of picture framing is now changing.

Logan Graphic Products, the worldwide leader in mat cutting equipment, has seen the trend and has now developed a full line of frame making equipment, which, in addition to their mat cutter line, provides small, start-up and do-it-yourself picture framers with the ability to produce quality framing without a disheartening outlay of cash and commitment. And Logan is not alone. In the same spirit other manufacturers have come to the fore, companies like Lineco, Inc. and Filmoplast, both purveyors of quality artwork mounting tapes, and 3M, Inc., the worldwide leader in mounting adhesives and tape application tools. All have as their goal the simple concept of making picture framing accessible to anyone who wants to do it.

So the trend toward picture framing for the small, start-up and do-it-yourself picture framer is well underway. For those seeking a professional picture framer to provide a high-end service, there are still plenty of them; but now, by virtue of those brave few who toughed it out and demonstrated the need, there are other, less expensive ways to frame as well.

CHAPTER ONE

Designing Your Picture Framing

Wait. Wait just one minute. Don't go out and buy that stuff. You'd be making a mistake. Resist the urge. Sit down and take a look at what you're framing. That's what it's all about. The art of picture framing is about the framing of art, so that's where it starts—not with the frame. One of the most common errors novice framers make is to buy the frame before they've done their planning, thinking that framing is a little like baking a cake: gather the ingredients, then follow a list of instructions. It's not. Every frame job is unique and has to be planned for individually, which means making decisions that will guide how you present a specific piece of artwork. You might look at the composition without regard to anything else, but often proper designing means more than just focusing on the artwork. It can, in addition, mean making the framed artwork fit into a particular setting. And this dual obligation helps narrow the parameters by which design decisions are made—which is a good thing. You will find that anything you do to narrow your design decisions makes them easier.

Reading the Artwork

There are over three hundred color choices in matboard alone. Add to that an almost limitless variety of frames and the potential combinations are virtually endless. Where do you start? Well, a good place is with the composition itself. First, you will want to "read" the artwork. What is its dominant color value? What is its dominant temperature? How would you characterize its style?

A color's value is where it falls on the white-to-black scale. When it falls more towards white, it's a tint; when it falls more towards black, it's a shade. In between are tones. Some artwork is composed primarily of tints, like scientific botanicals, pastel prints and watercolors. Other artwork is composed primarily of shades like deep-hued sunsets or dark and brooding expressions rendered in oils. Often it is possible to look at a given artwork and detect its dominant value. When

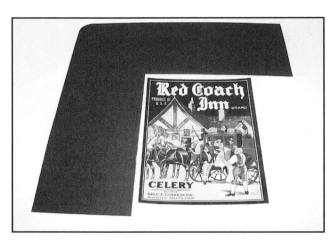

Figure A-1: The dominant value of this artwork consists primarily of shades, so the framing should also consist primarily of shades.

selecting colors for your framed presentation you will want to select colors that share the composition's dominant value (Figure A-1).

A composition's temperature is the predominance in the piece of either warm or cool colors. Warm colors are oranges, reds, yellows, browns, golds—the colors of autumn. Cool colors are violets, blues, greens, pinks—the colors of spring. Naturally, the composition will have a mix of colors, but you will be looking for the temperature that predominates. When selecting colors for

Figure A-2: Honoring the dominant temperature of the artwork means letting cool colors enhance a cool composition.

Contemporary artwork is enhanced by flat or box mouldings. Selecting a frame moulding that shares the style of the artwork is a key ingredient to effective presentation and is a major part of "reading" the artwork (Figure A-3).

But what if your reading of the artwork is different than that of someone else? Not to worry. The way you read the artwork is uniquely yours. You must have the courage and confidence to go forward with your interpretation. At the end of the day the framing of art is an art itself. At some point the framer's interpretation of the art's message and purpose must come into play, and it's unlikely that any two framers will interpret a composition exactly the same. But that doesn't mean that one or the other is wrong, just that each have a different set of parameters when it comes to evaluating the art's meaning. Designing well means, first, defining your parameters for a given piece of artwork, and then following the parameters you've laid out. Picture framing is not following a pre-set recipe; it's like creating a recipe yourself.

your framed presentation you will want to select colors that share the artwork's dominant temperature (Figure A-2).

In addition to value and temperature you will want to consider the style of the composition. Is it Contemporary? Classical? Rustic? Pastoral? Modern? Does it strike you as a slice of Americana or is it richly ethnic? Does it evoke bright, positive, upbeat feelings, or dark and brooding ones? The question of style is particularly relevant to the selection of a frame. The contoured and finished length of wood that will be your frame is referred to as a moulding. Highly ornamented frame mouldings do justice to Classical artwork. Streamlined mouldings in solid colors best enhance compositions with a Modern feel. Rustic or pastoral compositions are complemented by wood mouldings—oak or maple, even barnwood.

Figure A-3: The question of style is particularly relevant to the selection of a frame.

Determining the Window Size

Once you have a settled on a reading of the artwork, you will want to decide how you are going to present it in the window of the mat. You can display the image exclusively in the window of the mat, covering up any unprinted area surrounding the image. Or you may elect to show some of the unprinted area surrounding the image. Alternatively you may decide to show the paper complete, which means you will show the edges of the paper inside the window of the mat.

Your decision should be based on stylistic considerations. For example, presenting only the image is a more contemporary approach evocative of artwork that spreads or "bleeds" to the edges of the paper. Presenting the image as well as the unprinted area surrounding it is a more traditional approach, frequently used with prints and essential when the print is signed and numbered below the image. Showing the paper complete is an approach frequently used when the paper lends value to the presentation, as with a handmade paper or a paper suggestive of the composition, such as a Japanese painting on rice paper or Egyptian hieroglyphs on papyrus.

When matting a bleed—that is, displaying only the image in the window of the mat—the window is generally a half inch smaller than the dimensions of the image. Therefore, if the image is 8"x10", the window size is 7-1/2"x9-1/2". By making the window smaller by a half inch on each dimension, the window's edges encroach on the edges of the image by a quarter inch at each edge; and if the image is the same size as the paper, this quarter inch is sufficient to hold the

Figure B-1: When matting a bleed, subtract a half inch from each of the image dimensions to get the window size.

paper in the window (Figure B-1).

When matting to display both the image and the unprinted area surrounding it, determining the size of the window is a simple matter of measuring the area that consists of the image plus the unprinted area surrounding it, and then cutting the mat's window to that size (Figure B-2). Thus, if the image is 8"x10" and you want to expose an additional half inch of surrounding area, the window size will be 8-1/2"x10-1/2"—an entirely different window size than would be called for if the same artwork was matted as a bleed.

When matting to display the paper complete in the window of the mat, the artwork is first mounted against a mat blank (Figure B-3). A mat blank is a piece of matboard that has been reduced from the full size sheet to the frame size but doesn't have a window cut in it. Artwork can be mounted against a mat blank for presentation without a window mat. Such a presentation is called a float because the artwork is suspended or "floated" against

Figure B-2: When matting to display both the image and the unprinted area, simply measure the area you want to display.

Figure B-3: When matting to display the paper complete, the artwork is first "float mounted" against a mat blank.

Figure B-4: A window mat is placed over the artwork. The window of the mat is larger than the artwork.

the mat blank and the means of holding it there are concealed behind the artwork.

When matting to display the paper complete, the framer first floats the artwork and then places a window mat over it (Figure B-4). In this case, the window of the mat is larger than the artwork so that the edges of the paper are revealed. In addition, a margin of the mat blank on which the artwork is mounted is revealed. The degree of this reveal is up to the individual, but let's say the image is 8"x10" and the paper is 10"x12" (meaning there is a 1" wide margin of unprinted area surrounding the image). To show the paper complete in the window of the mat with a half-inch wide reveal of the mat blank along each edge, the window size will be 11"x13".

The point is, the way you decide to present the artwork in the window of the mat impacts the size of the window, and since measuring for matting and framing requires us to build from the artwork size outward to the frame size, the first step in the measuring process is to determine the window size. The next step is to determine the sizes of the mat borders that will surround the window. And then, by adding mat borders to the window size, you arrive at the frame size. This process will be detailed below. But for purposes of measuring it's very important to note that the frame size is not actually the size of the frame when measured from edge to edge but rather is the size of the recess within the frame that will accept the framing components. As a result, the perimeter sizes of the mat, backing board and glass are all the same size as the frame. Hence, working outward to the perimeter size of the mat is the same thing as working outward to the size of the frame.

Determining the Frame Size

The question frequently arises, "How do I know what mat borders will look right with the size window I've got?" To help answer that question, we've devised a table called the Border Finder (Figure C-1). Using the Border Finder, you will select borders that will look appropriate for the size window you've got. However, these may not be the borders you finally settle on. In most cases, given borders you know will look right, you will want to expand or contract them to fit a frame size that works for you. So this becomes a two-step process.

To use the Border Finder you must first express the window size in "united inches". The united inches of any two-dimensional object are the sum of the two dimensions. For example, the united inches of 16"x 20" is 16" + 20". In other words, 36 united inches. The united inches of 8"x 10" is 18 united inches.

Instructions - Border Finder

Using the Border Finder, find your sum in the table. (When the united inches falls between two numbers shown, use the higher number.) Then refer to the adjoining column to find appropriate borders for that size window. For example, for a window size of 8"x 10" we find that borders of 1-3/4" will be appropriate. This means four borders each of 1-3/4". (The question of whether the bottom border should be wider will enter our thinking a little further on.)

Adding the mat borders to each dimension of the window gives you the frame size. For example, adding two mat borders of 1-3/4" to each dimension of an 8"x 10" window gives you a frame size of 11-1/2"x 13-1/2".

Since it is always easier to work in whole inches rather than fractions, you will probably want to expand the mat borders a little to attain a whole-inch frame size. By adding a quarter inch to each mat border, you will add a half inch to the mat perimeter size, as well as to the frame size. Given our window size of 8"x 10", four borders of 2" will bring us to a frame size of 12"x 14".

Ah, but what if we want a wider bottom border? The rationale for a wider bottom border goes back to the nineteenth century when the style of hanging artwork was to hang it above eye level and have it pitch outward from the wall on a long wire so that viewing it required looking up from an angle. The wider bottom border was used to offset the illusion of imbalance inherent in this short-lived style of display, but the wider bottom border remains with us today because of its usefulness in making non-proportional art fit standard frames.

When the framer is obliged to use a predetermined frame size, as is the case when using frames made in standard sizes, using a wider bottom border helps to fit the frame (Figure C-2).

In our example, we have an 8"x 10" image surrounded by four borders of 2" which brings us to a frame size of 12"x 14"— but the closest standard frame size to that is 11"x 14". If we want to fit an 11"x 14" frame, the side borders will each have to be a half inch narrower (1-1/2"). The top border can be made slightly wider at 1-3/4", which will allow for the bottom border to be noticeably wider (2-1/4").

This "weighted border" effect is best used with compositions that benefit from sitting down in the frame or having a foundation or base. Landscapes are particularly well suited for wider bottom borders, as

Figure C-1: BORDER FINDER

BORDER FINDER

Instructions

Step 1. Convert your window dimensions to United Inches. To get the United Inches, simply add the height and the width. For example, the United Inches of a window that is 8"x10" is 18" (8" + 10" = 18").

Step 2. Find the United Inches of your Window Size in the first column. When the United Inches exceed the number shown, go to the next highest number. Read across to find your suggested Starting Borders.

Window Size in United Inches	Suggested Starting Borders	Window Size in United Inches	Suggested Starting Borders
6"	3/4"	38"	2 1/2"
8"	1"	40"	2 1/2"
10"	1 1/2"	42"	2 3/4"
12"	1 3/4"	44"	2 3/4"
14"	1 3/4"	46"	3"
16"	1 3/4"	48"	3"
18"	1 3/4"	50"	3"
20"	1 3/4"	52"	3"
22"	1 3/4"	54"	3 1/4"
24"	1 3/4"	56"	3 1/4"
26"	2"	58"	3 1/4"
28"	2"	60"	3 1/2"
30"	2"	62"	3 1/2"
32"	2"	64"	3 1/2"
34"	2 1/4"	66"	3 3/4"
36"	2 1/4"	68"	3 3/4"

are portraits and other artwork with a distinct horizon.

But what if we prefer all four borders the same? By being able to make our own frames, we will not be forced into using a wider bottom border when we don't really want one. By being able to make our own frames, we can make all four borders the same because we can make the frame any size we want it.

Measuring for Frame Making

Getting the measurements correct for frame making is a bit more complicated than it appears at first. The first-time framer can be forgiven for believing that making, say, a 12"x14" frame involves nothing more than cutting two 12" moulding sections and two 14" moulding sections and assembling them. Such an approach would quickly run aground because the framer would be overlooking a number of important details.

As was mentioned earlier, the perimeter size of the frame (i.e., the frame measured from edge to edge) is not 12"x14". Rather, it's the recess at the back of the frame (the part that contains the stack of mat, artwork, backing and glass) that is 12"x14". Framers refer to this recess as the "rabbet" (Figure D-1). Also, in order to make a 90-degree corner, the ends of each section must be cut at an angle. When two of these 45-degree angles are fitted together, they form a 90-degree corner. The 45-degree cuts at the ends of each section are called "miters" (Figure D-2) and the tool necessary to cut them is a miter saw. But when measuring to cut a miter, you must measure

Figure C-2: Using a wider bottom border allows a framer to fit a frame.

Figure D-1: The frame size is the interior recess of the frame which is called the "rabbet."

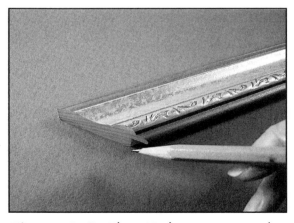

Figure D-2: The 45-degree cut at the end of each section is called the "miter."

from the outside edge of the miter, not the inside. So what exactly is the measurement at the outside edge of the miter, because as we've said it's not 12"x 14"?

The measurement at the outside edge of the miter is the length of the section plus the width of the frame when measured across its face (Figure D-3). And since there are miters at both ends of each section, to determine the measurement of each frame section, including its miters, you must add the width of the frame twice to the length. So, let's say you want to make a 12"x 14" frame from a moulding that's 1-1/2" wide. The measurement for each 12" section will be 12" + (2 x 1-1/2 ") or 12" + 3" = 15". The measurement for each 14" section will be 14" + (2 x 1-1/2") or 14" + 3" = 17". The measurement will of course be different if the width of the moulding is different.

Having said this, we're not finished yet. If we create the above frame, using the measurements indicated, we will indeed have a frame that's 12"x 14"—but it will end up being exactly 12"x 14". What if we make a mistake and find ourselves a fraction of an inch off? The stack of mat, artwork, backing and glass won't fit! And indeed if we make a mistake cutting any one of the framing components, we're in trouble. Smart framers build an "allowance" into their frame providing extra clearance should anything not be exact. This allowance is typically 1/8". So now the proper equation for determining frame size is length of section + width of frame (x 2) + 1/8". Looking at the 12"x 14" we're talking about:

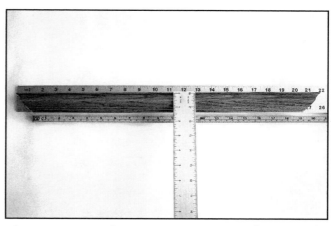

Figure D-3: The measurement at the outside edge of the miter is the length of the section plus the width of the frame x 2.

$$12" + (2 \times 1\text{-}1/2") + 1/8" = 15\text{-}1/8"$$

and

$$14" + (2 \times 1\text{-}1/2") + 1/8" = 17\text{-}1/8"$$

Mind you, you will need two sections of each length to make the frame, so you will need 64 1/2" of moulding to make the above frame. Here's how we figured that:

$$15\text{-}1/8" + 15\text{-}1/8" + 17\text{-}1/8" + 17\text{-}1/8"$$
$$= 64\text{-}1/2"$$

But moulding is not sold in inches. It's sold in feet. So to know how long a piece of moulding is needed, we'll have to convert the inches to feet. No problem. There are 12 inches to each foot, so we'll divide the inches by 12 to get our feet: 64-1/2" divided by 12 is 5 feet, 4-1/2 inches. We'll need a stick of moulding 5 feet, 4-1/2" long. But moulding is only sold in feet. So we'll need a stick of moulding 6 feet long to make this 12"x 14" frame.

As you can see, there will be almost a full foot of moulding left over after we make the frame—a full foot of scrap. But don't feel bad about that. Bear in mind, you are saving in the neighborhood of 75 percent by making this frame yourself, even with the scrap! Not only that, but you may need the extra moulding in order to make the frame out of two 4-foot sections, rather than one 8-foot section. The problem is, shipping anything longer than 6 feet increases its cost. Therefore, unless the manufacturer of the moulding can deliver the stick locally, it behooves him to sell it in shorter lengths. Consequently, most moulding is sold in 3-foot, 4-foot or 5-foot lengths, which means that when you make a frame you must select the correct lengths.

Let's look at the possibilities given the 64-1/2" necessary to make our 12"x 14":

4 feet is 48 inches. We can get both 17-1/8" sections out of 48" with 13" of moulding left over, but that won't be enough to get even one section of 15-1/8". This approach produces a lot of scrap.

5 feet is 60 inches. We can get both 17-1/8" sections out of 60" with enough moulding left over to make one section of 15-1/8". But that means we'll have to buy a separate 3-foot length to get the remaining 15-1/8" section. If we have to buy two lengths of moulding, it will be preferable to buy two of the shorter lengths than one long one and one short one? Let's look at the final option.

Three feet is 36 inches. We can get both of the 15-1/8" sections out of 36". We can also get both of the 17-1/8" sections out of a second 36". So the most economical approach is to make our 12"x 14" out of two 3-foot lengths of moulding.

Now it's just a matter of buying the two 3-foot sticks of moulding and getting to work.

CHAPTER TWO

Preparing Your Framing Materials

When you begin your picture framing project, many of the materials you will use are not in the condition necessary to use them. For example, at this stage your frame moulding is a pair of sticks, not a picture frame. Your matboard and backing are 32"x40" sheets, not even reduced to frame size. And your glass or acrylic may be too large. Before going any further you need to reduce your materials to size. Armed with the notes you took during the measuring and designing stage of the process, you are ready to proceed.

Cutting Picture Frame Moulding

One of the most challenging parts of picture framing is building a frame with joints that close tightly in the corners with no gaps or discrepancies. One of the essential steps to achieving this is to saw the miters accurately. To make a frame with four 90-degree corners you are going to need to cut eight 45-degree miters. Each one of these miters must be virtually flawless. If any one is even slightly off a gap will appear at the joint. For this reason you must have as much accuracy in sawing as you can reasonably afford.

Beware of inexpensive miter boxes and manual saws. Generally these tools do not provide enough accuracy for picture framing. Plastic and wooden miter boxes are always to be avoided. Manual miter saws can, with practice, produce adequate results, but they will usually require sanding after the fact to close the joints.

In considering a miter saw for picture framing also bear in mind that there are two kinds of moulding: softwood mouldings and hardwood mouldings. While sawing softwood mouldings with a manual saw is easy enough, sawing hardwood mouldings can be quite demanding. Most softwood mouldings can be sawed through in nine or ten strokes. Sawing through hardwood of comparable thickness may require as many as thirty strokes.

What's more, the rigorous back and forth raking action of a manual saw can lead to blade twist or blade torque, resulting in less than accurate miters.

For all these reasons, it is advisable to use a power saw when cutting picture frame moulding. A power miter saw can cut through hardwood or softwood with ease, and the quality of the cut is generally better than that produced by a manual saw. Which is not to say that you will never have to sand your miters if you use a power saw. For a variety of reasons – warped mouldings, intrusive ornamentation, uneven expansion through the stick – discrepancies at the joint remain a possibility and sanding should be viewed as an inevitable part of the frame making process. But more frequent and consistent accuracy is attained with a power saw than with a manual saw.

Most power miter saws, however, are designed for the building trades and lack some of the essential ease-of-use features to be found in a good picture framing saw. Fortunately, these features can be added after the fact.

For example, most power miter saws do not come outfitted with the correct blade. In picture framing, an 80-tooth blade is necessary to provide the sort of fine cuts needed to close eight miter faces. Most power miter saws come with 40-tooth blades. Replace the 40-tooth blade with an 80-tooth blade

Figure E-1: Set the pivot of your miter saw to 45-degrees on the right.

of the saw, and the remaining 4-1/2 feet of moulding where? Hanging out in space?

A proper 3 foot fence extension provides support for the rest of the moulding and provides a way of measuring the moulding while it's in the saw. A fence extension with an angled scale is best. Such a scale is unique because the increments are at 45-degrees, not at 90-degrees as is the case with most scales. The 45-degree scale is pertinent to picture framing because the frame size – the size you are measuring – is not the outside dimension of the frame. As mentioned before, the frame size is considered to be the size of the recess at the back of the frame,

purchased separately to make your miter saw picture frame ready. Note that you can select a blade with more than 80 teeth if you like. The more the better. But the blade should not have less than 80 teeth.

Another feature you will want is a picture framing saw fence extension. Power miter saws typically offer little in the way of a proper fence extension, perhaps just a thin bar that extends six inches on either side of the saw deck. Without an extension for the fence of your miter saw you must contrive a way to support the majority of the stick while sawing it. Quite often you are cutting just a few inches from the end of a long stick to produce a miter, which means you may have only three inches through the saw gap, maybe six inches more on the deck

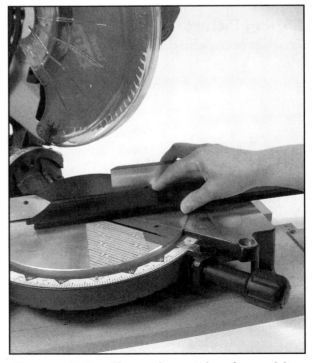

Figure E-2: Place the stick of moulding against the saw fence finished side up with the rabbet facing toward you.

Figure E-3: Move the moulding just past the slot in the saw fence so a 45-degree cut can be made at the end of the stick.

Figure E-4: Hold the moulding firmly against the fence, activate the saw & lower the blade through the wood.

what picture framers call the rabbet.

Seen as a single side of the frame with the miters already cut, the frame size is not the length of the stick measured to the two points of the miter. The frame size is the length of the stick measured to the two inside points of the miter. The only way to measure accurately to those points is with a scale having increments at 45-degrees.

Finally, a proper fence extension comes with a stop which can be used to position the moulding precisely on the scale for making repeated cuts of the same length.

To cut the moulding, begin by cutting the two long sections first. If a mistake is made, the two shorter pieces can still be salvaged out of the longer pieces you made a mistake on.

STEP ONE: Set the pivot of your miter saw to 45-degrees on the right (Figure E-1).

STEP TWO: Place the stick of moulding against the saw fence. It's important to place the moulding on the fence correctly. The moulding should be finished side up with the rabbet facing toward you (Figure E-2).

STEP THREE: To begin you are going to cut a miter at one end of the stick. Move the moulding past the saw gap, enough so that a 45-degree cut can be made at the end of the stick (Figure E-3).

STEP FOUR: Hold the moulding firmly against the saw fence, activate the power saw blade and lower the blade through the wood (Figure E-4).

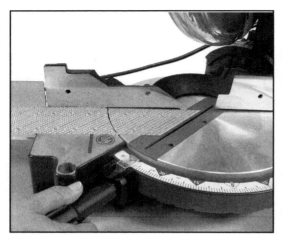

Figure E-5: Set the pivot of your miter saw to 45-degrees on the left.

STEP FIVE: For the second cut, set the pivot of your miter saw to 45-degrees on the left (Figure E-5).

STEP SIX: Place the moulding you just cut against the saw fence finished side up with the rabbet facing toward you. Move the moulding down the scale until the inside corner of the miter is at the measurement that denotes the size you wish to cut (Figure E-6).

STEP SEVEN: Move the fence stop against the moulding. Let the moulding seat itself within the gap at the back of the stop. Tighten the fence stop into position (Figure E-7).

STEP EIGHT: Activate the power saw and lower the blade through the wood. After cutting, leave the stop where it is. One section of the frame is done.

STEP NINE: For the next section, return your miter saw to 45-degrees on the right. Place the second stick of moulding against the saw fence so the finished side is up and the rabbet facing toward you (Figure E-8). Move the moulding just past the saw gap, enough so that a 45-degree cut can be made at the end of the stick. Cut the moulding.

Figure E-6: Move the moulding down the scale until the inside corner of the miter is at the proper measurement.

Figure E-7: Let the moulding seat itself within the gap at the back of the stop.

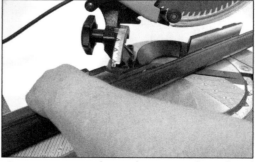

Figure E-8: Place the second stick of moulding against the fence so the finished side is up and the rabbet facing toward you.

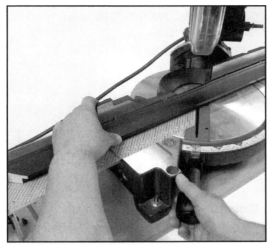

Figure E-9: Move the moulding along the scale until it lines up at the precise measurement.

Figure E-10: Let the moulding seat within the gap at the back of the fence stop.

Figure F-1: A strap clamp is the best way to see the frame fully assembled before driving nails into it.

STEP TEN: To complete the next section, move the saw back to 45-degrees on the left. Move the moulding back along the fence (Figure E-9). Bring the moulding into contact with the stop (Figure E-10). Cut the moulding.

STEP ELEVEN: Repeat the above procedure for the remaining two frame sections.

STEP TWELVE: To check the precision of your work, lay two frame sections of equal length on their side with the miters facing up. Align the miters at one end. Run a finger across the surface of the two miters to be sure they are flush. Then check the miters at the other end of the two sticks in the same way. They also should be flush. If not, the cut may not have been precise and sanding may be required. This is not uncommon. Sanding is routinely required when making frames. But the job can be done quickly and accurately with the right tool.

Sanding Picture Frame Moulding

A more precise way to ascertain the precision of your miter cuts prior to sanding is to employ a strap clamp (sometimes called a band clamp). Using a strap clamp allows you to see your frame fully assembled with all the miters firmly in contact before you begin nailing. When the frame is in the strap clamp it will be clear if there are any gaps or discrepancies at the joints that require sanding (Figure F-1).

Logan offers the Model F200-2 Sander to make the job of sanding quick, simple and precise.

STEP ONE: Set the alignment bar of the sander at 45-degrees (Figure F-2).

STEP TWO: Place the frame section to be corrected against the alignment bar so the finished side is up and the rabbet is facing toward the center of the sanding disc.

STEP THREE: Hold the moulding so it presses against the alignment bar and bring the miter face firmly against the surface of the sanding disc (Figure F-3).

Rotate the sanding disc. The disc should always rotate downward onto the top of the moulding (Figure F-4). Rotate the disc four to six times. Do not press too hard. It is better to have more rotations as opposed to harder pressure.

Check your progress by placing the two sections on their backs side by side with the miters facing up and running a finger across the surface of the two miters, or for better precision use a strap clamp. Repeat the above procedure for the other two sections and you are ready to join your frame.

Reducing Matboard and Foamboard to Frame Size

Matboard is usually sold in sheets of 32"x40" which you will need to reduce to

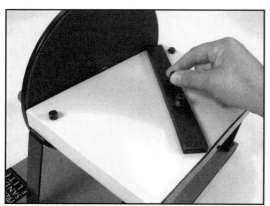

Figure F-2: Set the alignment bar of the sander at 45-degrees.

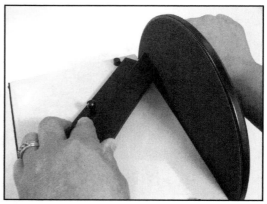

Figure F-3: Press the miter face against the disc.

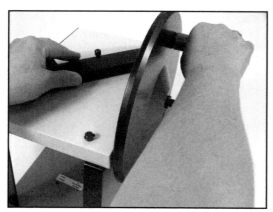

Figure F-4: The disc should always rotate downward on top of the moulding.

Figure G-1: A squaring arm provides an abutment against which the sheet rests during cutting.

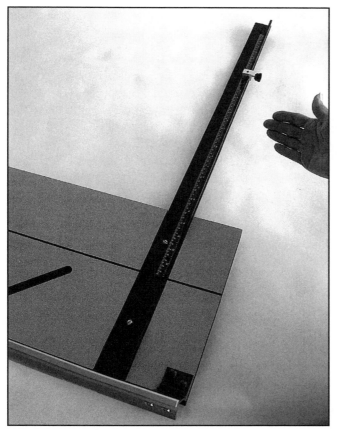

Figure G-2: The squaring arm sticks out at right angle from bed of mat cutter, providing a scale for measuring.

G-1). Since the squaring arm is situated at a precise right angle to the guide rail of the mat cutter, all cuts made with the matboard abutted against the squaring arm will be square.

A squaring arm is different than a squaring bar, which acts as an abutment but provides no means of measuring. A squaring arm sticks out at a right angle from the bed of the mat cutter and provides a scale on which to measure (Figure G-2). Three full size Logan mat cutters include squaring arms: the Logan Model 750 Simplex Plus Mat Cutter, the Logan Model 650 Framer's Edge Mat Cutter, and the Logan 850 Platinum Edge Mat Cutter.

To reduce matboard to size using a squaring arm, begin by removing the mat guide of your mat cutter (Figure G-3). Then lift the guide rail of the mat cutter and insert the full sheet of matboard. Place the bottom edge of the sheet firmly against the squaring arm and move the right edge to the right until

your desired size. Cutting it precisely to size is important, because matboard that is inaccurately sized is usually out of square, meaning that it is not cut at proper right angles. This will cause problems later when you cut a window in it or when you place it in your frame.

Reducing matboard accurately to size can be achieved with due care in measuring, marking and cutting, but the process can be simplified with the use of a squaring arm. A squaring arm provides an abutment against which the edge of the sheet rests during cutting (Figure

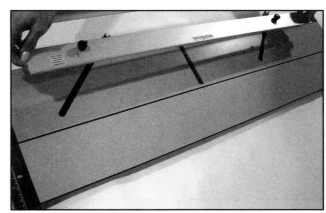

Figure G-3: Remove the mat guide

Figure G-4: Move the right edge to the right until it aligns with the proper measurement on the squaring arm scale.

it aligns with the size you want (Figure G-4). Lower the guide rail.

Adjust your 90-degree cutting head to penetrate four-ply (single thickness) matboard. Situate the cutting head outside the top edge of the matboard so the blade sits in the slot in the cutting bed (Figure G-5). Pull back toward you, cutting the sheet (Figure G-6). As you cut, the action of pulling brings the bottom edge of the sheet firmly against the squaring arm, keeping the mat square. Cut through the bottom edge of the sheet. The squaring arm has a slot in it to let the blade pass through.

To cut the second dimension, turn the sheet a quarter turn. Again place the bottom edge against the squaring arm and move the right edge along the scale until it aligns with the size you want. Cut again and your

Figure G-5: Situate the cutting head outside the top edge of the matboard.

Figure G-6: Pull back toward you, cutting the sheet.

matboard is accurately sized.

The Logan Model 450-1 Artist Elite Mat Cutter includes a squaring bar and a measuring bar. To size using this mat cutter, install the measuring bar Into the machine, insert the mat blank and rest the edge of the mat board blank on the measuring bar number you wish to size the blank to. The Model 450-1 includes a 90-degree cutting head with adjustable blade depth to make this straight cut.

The Logan Model 301-1 Compact Classic Mat Cutter has no squaring feature but the capacity of its cutting bed is 32". To reduce mat board to size using this mat cutter, you must insert the 32" side of the mat board into the machine and using a ruler or measuring tape, mark out the back of the mat blank to the size you wish to cut it to.

The Logan Model 350-1 Compact Elite Mat Cutter includes a squaring bar and a measuring bar with a stop. It also has a 32" capacity like the model 301-1 Compact Classic. But with the use of the measuring bar, you can size mat blanks much faster than the 301-1 can.

To reduce matboard to size using a hand-held mat cutter instead of a mat cutting system, you should use a Logan Model 500 Mat Knife, a rule and a straightedge. First, measure and mark the sheet for the size you want, then align a straightedge along the mark and score the line. Avoid trying to cut through the sheet in one pass, instead score repeatedly—as many as three or four times—to insure a clean cut (Figure G-7).

The procedure for reducing foamboard to size is exactly the same as for reducing matboard except that the depth of the blade in the 90-degree cutter should be set at its lowest setting. Foamboard is best sized in a mat cutter that includes a 90-degree cutting head with an adjustable depth. It is problematic to attempt reducing foamboard with just a mat knife or utility knife. If you must reduce foamboard by hand, use the Logan Foamboard Cutter, Model 1500 (Figure

Figure G-7: To size outside a mat cutter, score repeatedly with your mat knife along the straightedge.

Figure G-8: Use the Logan Foamboard Cutter to size foamboard manually.

G-8), designed for this purpose.

Reducing Glass to Size

Like matboard and foamboard, glass can be quickly and accurately sized with a squaring arm. The measuring feature of the squaring arm is particularly pertinent when cutting glass because, unlike matboard and foamboard, it is difficult to mark the surface of glass, and since the use of a squaring arm eliminates the need for marking, the procedure is greatly simplified. Logan makes the Model 704 Glass Cutter which adapts to the Model 750 Simplex Plus Mat

Figure H-1: Cover the bed of your mat cutter with a backing sheet.

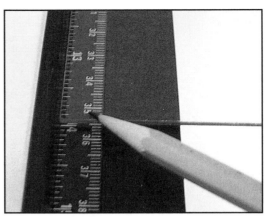

Figure H-2: Move the right edge of the glass to the right until it lines up with the correct point on the scale.

Figure H-3: Hook the glass cutter onto outermost lip of the guide rail.

Cutter, the Model 450 Intermediate Mat Cutter and the Model 301-1 and 350-1 Compact Mat Cutters.

Before attempting to cut glass on your Model 750 Simplex Plus Mat Cutter, cut a piece of scrap matboard just wide enough to cover the bed (Figure H-1). Cutting glass involves the deposit of glass dust and particles; the piece of scrap matboard prevents these from getting into the slots and channels of your mat cutter. In addition, it is advisable to wear white cotton gloves when cutting and handling glass.

To cut glass, remove the mat guide of your mat cutter, lift the guide rail and place the glass on the cutting bed. Place the bottom edge of the glass firmly against the squaring arm and move the right edge to the right until it aligns with the size you want (Figure H-2). Lower the guide rail.

Figure H-4: Pull the glass cutter back, scoring the surface of the glass.

Place the Model 704 Glass Cutter on the guide rail just outside the top edge of the glass (Figure H-3). Bring the cutter into position so the cutting wheel is resting against the edge of the glass. Squirt a small bead of glass cutting fluid along the proposed line of the cut. Exert slight downward pressure on the cutter and pull back, scoring the surface of the glass (Figure H-4). Unlike cutting matboard or foamboard, where you cut through the material in one pass, cutting glass is a matter of scoring and snapping. After scoring, remove the glass from the cutter and bring it to the edge of a table or counter top. Align the score along the edge and press down, snapping the glass cleanly along the score (Figure H-5).

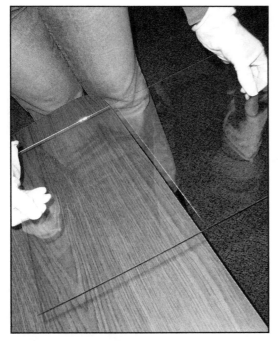

Figure H-5: Align the score along the edge of the table and snap the glass cleanly along the score.

CHAPTER THREE

Assembling Your Picture Frame

After you've prepared your materials, it's time to fashion them into something you can actually use. For matting this means cutting a window in the mat blank. For framing this means taking the frame sections you've cut from the longer sticks and assembling them into an actual frame by joining them at the corners.

Logan offers two joiners for assembling picture frame mouldings: The Studio Joiner F300-1 clamps the moulding in a standard clamp (included) and presses one V-nail at a time into the back of the frame with the moulding lying face down. The Pro Joiner F300-2 clamps the frame in a sophisticated vise and drives two V-nails up from under with the moulding lying face up. The less expensive Studio Joiner requires you to visually line up the nails before driving. The Pro Joiner aligns the nails for you, making the process quicker and more precise.

A "V-nail" is a V-shaped staple designed to penetrate the wood at the joint where the mitered ends of two frame sections come together to form a corner (Figure I-1). V-nailing is preferred over traditional nailing because the nail is driven into the back of the moulding rather than through the side, making it less conspicuous and avoiding the need to cosmetically cover up the nail head.

Joining with the Studio Joiner F300-1:

Step One: Begin by selecting the correct V-nail for the job. V-nails commonly come in two types (hardwood or soft/medium wood) and three sizes (1/4", 3/8" or 1/2"). Hardwood V-nails are often red along the cutting edge while soft/medium V-nails are often white along the cutting edge. Hardwood V-nails should be used for very hard woods like oak, hickory and maple. Soft/medium wood V-nails should be used for most other types of moulding, including

Figure I-1: A V-nail is a V-shaped staple that penetrates the wood on either side of the miter.

Figure I-2: Mark edge of each miter to hide any gap in the joint.

Figure I-3: Place a small bead of wood glue on the face of the miter.

Figure I-4: Press the spring button and slide the clamp handle forward, trapping the moulding.

Figure I-5: Adjust the joint so the two miters are aligned.

pine and basswood. The size of the V-nail indicates the depth to which the V-nail will sink into the wood, not the width across its wings. Choose a V-nail that is slightly more than half the thickness of the moulding. For example, if you have a moulding that measures 3⁄4" thick, a 1⁄2" V-nail would be best. Plan on using two V-nails per joint unless the frame is very narrow.

STEP TWO: If you wish, before clamping the moulding, you can mark the edge of each miter with a stain pencil to disguise any gap at the joint and render the seam inconspicuous (Figure I-2). The corners of frames joined by V-nails should always be reinforced with wood glue. Gluing is as important in building a sturdy frame as nailing. Place a small bead of wood glue on the miter face of one section and spread it evenly over the miter before clamping (Figure I-3).

STEP THREE: Select two moulding sections to join. Unless the frame is square-shaped, this means one section will be longer than the other. Put the longer section on the right and the shorter section on the left as you place them in the clamp.

STEP FOUR: Place the two sections face up in the clamp. Bring the two miters into contact with each other. Press the spring button and slide the clamp handle forward, trapping the two sections (Figure I-4). Wipe away any excess glue that squeezes out at the seam. Use a wet cloth followed by a dry cloth for quick, thorough clean up.

STEP FIVE: Loosen the clamp slightly and adjust the joint so the two miters are aligned, making a perfect corner (Figure I-5). Re-tighten the clamp firmly.

Figure I-6: Raise the beam so the clamped moulding will fit under it.

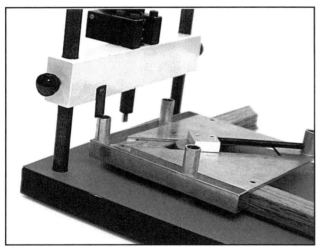

Figure I-7: Lower the beam until the depth gauge touches the top of one of the posts.

STEP SIX: Adjust the beam height for depth of penetration. Loosen the knobs on either end of the beam and raise the beam so the clamped moulding will fit under it (Figure I-6). Turn the clamped frame over so the ornamented side of the moulding is down. The clamp has legs on the bottom that stick up when the clamped frame is turned over. Slide the clamped moulding under the beam, lower the beam until the depth gauge touches the top of one of the legs (Figure I-7). Then tighten the knobs, fixing the beam in place. The depth gauge may be pivoted out of the way after this for added clearance.

STEP SEVEN: Determine whether or not to use the spacer. Mouldings likely to tip or rock when lying face down will need the spacer to level and support them (Figure I-8). With the clamped moulding face down, insert the spacer between the moulding and the base if necessary (Figure I-9).

STEP EIGHT: Load a V-nail. Hardwood V-nails are red along the edge while soft/medium V-nails are white. The colored edge is the sharp edge. It is important that the

Figure I-8: Mouldings prone to rock will need the spacer to support them.

Figure I-9: Insert the spacer between the clamped moulding and the base.

Figure I-10: Load the V-nail onto the magnetic tip with the sharp/colored edge facing down.

Figure I-11: Visually align the penetration point of the V-nail.

V-nail be driven with the cutting edge against the wood. Driving a V-nail upside down will cause it to jam and crumple. Place the V-nail on the magnetic nose that protrudes from the black cylinder under the beam with the sharp edge facing down. (Figure I-10).

STEP NINE: Visually align the penetration point of the V-nail. Place the first V-nail about a quarter inch in from the rabbet. Place the second V-nail about halfway between the first V-nail and the perimeter of the frame (Figure I-11). The wings of the V-nail should penetrate evenly on either side of the joint.

STEP TEN: Press down on the lever, driving the V-nail into the wood (Figure I-12). Press until the bottom of the V-nail is flush with the surface of the wood. Repeat for the second V-nail on the same corner.

Repeat for the remaining three corners of the frame. Be careful when assembling the remaining sides. Instead of adding another section to the sections already joined, join the remaining two sections next. If you started by placing the long length on the right side of the vise, then the second half of the frame must also be joined by placing the long length on the right side of the vise, thereby giving you two identical halves of a frame which can be correctly joined together.

Joining with the Pro Joiner F300-2:

STEP ONE: The clamp moves up and down for an adjustable height relative to the base of the joiner. Lock the clamp at a level that's easy to work with using the clamp locking collar (Figure J-1).

Figure I-12: Press down on the lever, driving the nail.

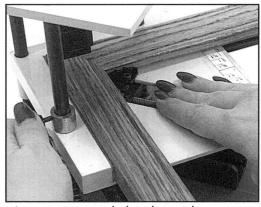

Figure J-1: Lock the clamp down using the clamp locking collar.

Figure J-2: Adjust the clamp jaw by pressing the spring button and sliding the handle until the moulding is secure.

Figure J-3: Adjust the moulding sections in the clamp so the top corner is square.

Figure J-4: Measure the width of the moulding using the set block scale on the clamp.

STEP TWO: Select two moulding sections to join. Unless the frame is square-shaped, this means one section will be longer than the other. Plan on putting the longer section on the right and shorter section on the left when you place them in the clamp.

Before putting the sections in the clamp you may want to mark the edge of each miter with a stain pencil to disguise any gap at the joint and render the seam inconspicuous. Glue the sections before clamping. The corners of frames joined by V-nails should always be reinforced with wood glue. Place a small bead of wood glue on the miter face of one section and spread it evenly. Place the two sections of moulding face up in the clamp. Bring the two miters into contact with each other. Press the spring button and slide the clamp jaw forward, trapping the two sections (Figure J-2).

STEP THREE: It's important to align the joint properly in the clamp. Loosen the clamp slightly and adjust the sections so the top corner of the joint is square (Figure J-3). Then re-tighten the clamp firmly.

STEP FOUR: Adjust the position of the V-nails. First, measure the width of the moulding using the set block scale on the clamp (Figure J-4).

STEP FIVE: Next, working from the measurement determined on the set block scale, adjust the V-nail blocks on the cartridge to that measurement (Figure J-5). Do not load the V-nails yet. First, you must

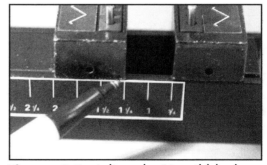

Figure J-5: Adjust the V-nail blocks to the measurement determined on the set block scale.

Figure J-6: Adjust the foot until it contacts the moulding.

Figure J-7: Slide the V-nail block cartridge (without the V-nails loaded) between the guides. Slide it back until it stops.

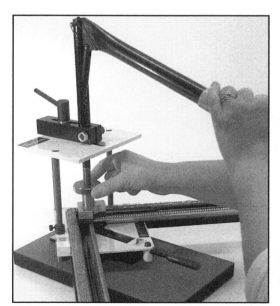

Figure J-8: Lower the lever arm and make minor adjustments to the foot level until the moulding bottoms out on the V-nail blocks.

adjust the range of the press.

STEP SIX: To adjust the range of the press, release the clamp locking collar and adjust the foot screw until the foot contacts the face of the moulding (Figure J-6).

STEP SEVEN: Slide the V-nail block cartridge (without the V-nails loaded) between the guides. Slide it back until it stops (Figure J-7).

STEP EIGHT: Lower the lever arm and make minor adjustments to the foot level by turning the foot screw (Figure J-8). Keep adjusting until the moulding bottoms out on the V-nail blocks when the lever arm is fully lowered. You will feel the lever arm notch and lock as it bottoms out. The range of the press is now adjusted and you are ready to load the V-nails.

STEP NINE: Raise the lever arm and remove the V-nail block cartridge. Load the V-nails onto the blocks. Make sure the sharp edge of each V-nail is up. It's important that the V-nail is driven with the cutting edge against the wood. Driving a V-nail upside down will cause it to jam and crumple. Small diagrams on the blocks will show you the proper arrangement of the V-nails on the pins (Figure J-9).

Figure J-9: Remove the V-nail block cartridge and load V-nails onto the V-nail blocks.

Figure J-10: Slide the V-nail block cartridge (with the V-nails loaded) between the guides. Slide it back until it stops.

Figure J-11: Lower the lever arm to drive the V-nails.

Figure J-12: The Pro-Joiner drives the V-nails flush with the surface of the wood.

STEP TEN: Slide the V-nail block cartridge (with the V-nails loaded) between the guides. Slide it back until it stops (Figure J-10).

STEP ELEVEN: Lower the lever arm to drive the V-nails (Figure J-11).

STEP TWELVE: The Pro Joiner drives the V-nails flush with the surface of the wood (Figure J-12). Clamp your next two moulding sections and repeat the driving procedure. There is no need to readjust the position of the V-nails or the range of the press until you change to a different width of moulding.

CHAPTER FOUR

Cutting Your Mat

Logan makes a wide range of mat cutters suitable for everyone from the novice to the professional. Which mat cutter is right for you depends on two of the following factors: how many mats you will be cutting on a weekly basis and how quickly you want to master your mat cutting skills.

Understanding the Differences Between Mat Cutters

Consider how much time you're willing to spend becoming proficient at mat cutting, because the learning curve does get progressively shorter the more you spend. On

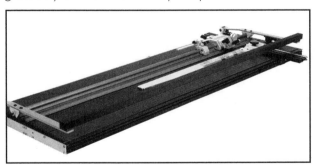

Figure K-1: High-end mat cutters like the Platinum Edge are designed for heavy duty frame shop use.

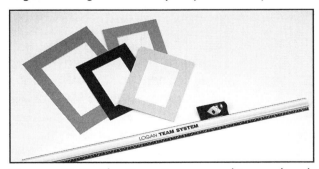

Figure K-2: The Team System combines a hand-held cutter with a guide rail.

the other hand, you don't have to empty your bank account to find a comfort zone. In fact, good mat cutting becomes a manageable proposition with the purchase of a mat cutter in the $75 to $500 price range, and does not get a whole lot easier even if you spend more.

High-end mat cutters, such as the Logan Platinum Edge, Model #850, are built to take the wear and tear of rigorous professional use, as is common in a frame shop. They have thicker, more durable cutting boards, heavier guide rails and bigger cutting heads. They are designed to cut 100+ mats a week, to stand up under continuous use and are production-oriented for multiple repeat cuts. They are easy to become comfortable with and provide consistently good results straight out of the box (Figure K-1).

On the other end of the spectrum, hand-held mat cutters are capable of cutting just about anything. With a hand-held cutter you can cut a window as precise as one cut on the world's most expensive mat cutter—but you'd better be willing to devote some time. The learning curve on hand-held cutters can be long. Hand-held cutters usually require a fair amount of patience to master.

A mat cutting "system" is distinguished from a hand-held mat cutter in that it provides some of the other necessities besides just the mat cutter, such as a place to cut (a cutting board), a measuring system, and a straightedge to cut against (a "guide rail"). A system such as the Logan Team System combines a hand-held mat cutter with a guide rail and allows the cutting head to ride on the guide rail to eliminate the problem of the two pushing against each other (Figure K-2). Still, the guide rail it-

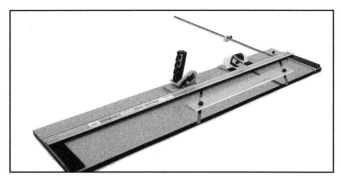

Figure K-3: The Logan Compact Elite Mat Cutter provides a fixed guide rail and built-in measuring system.

self is not attached to anything and may slip, even though it has a rubberized base.

Systems that have the guide rail attached to the base board, or board-mounted mat cutters as they are called, represent a vast improvement. The Compact Mat Cutters are this type of mat cutter. For those serious about cutting mats, a 32" capacity mat cutting system like the 301-1 Compact Classic or 350-1 Compact Elite represents the minimal investment for the quick attainment of superior mat cutting skills.

On the face of it, the biggest shortcoming of a 32" mat cutter appears to be its size. After all, a sheet of mat board is 32"x 40". So right away you might conclude that with a 32" mat cutter, large mats can't be cut. But this is not so. 32" mat cutters are open at either end so the mat board can shift along the cutting board to allow for cutting a window of any size. However, it is true that the small size of a 32" mat cutter requires special attention when it comes to sizing. Sizing means reducing a full size sheet of mat board to the frame size. A 32" capacity mat cutter like the 301-1 or 350-1 can only accept the 32" side of a full sheet of mat board, not the 40" side.

The Logan Compact Elite Mat Cutter Model 350-1 has the same 32" size capacity as the Logan Compact Classic model 301-1. However it has some handy additions like a squaring bar to hold mat board square

and a measuring bar which speeds up downsizing of mat blanks. Plus it has production stops to speed repeat cuts and a regular pull style straight cutter instead of a hand-held mat knife (Figure K-3).

The next grade of mat cutters solves this problem of working with full 32" x 40" mat board with no limitations. Mat cutters such as the Logan Model 450-1 Artist Elite Mat Cutter provide a full 40" base board with a hinging guide rail, squaring bar, measuring bar, production stops plus bevel and straight cutting heads. And it accepts a full sheet of 32"x40" mat board with ease.

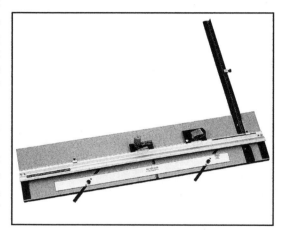

Figure K-4: The Simplex is a full-featured mat cutter, including a squaring arm, a 40-1/2" cutting bed and production stops.

The Logan Model 750 Simplex is another example. It is a full-featured mat cutter that includes a host of innovative benefits, including all those listed above, plus production stops and the durability to handle an average of 25+ mats per week (Figure K-4).

Mat Cutters above the 750 Simplex, like the Model 850 Platinum Edge Mat Cut-

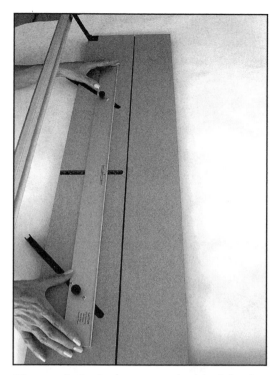

Figure L-1: By loosening the black knobs, you can slide the mat guide back and forth.

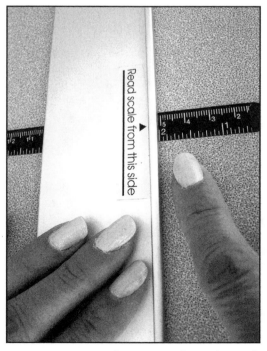

Figure L-2: Set the mat guide on the scale for the border you want to cut.

ter, are considered production cutters designed to cut hundreds of mats a day if necessary with great precision and efficiency, ideal for frame shops or contract framing.

In choosing a mat cutter, the wise shopper weighs the advantages of each against budget and makes an informed decision. Good mat cutting begins with a good tool—and one that's right for you.

Cutting a Single Mat

Cutting a single mat is a three-step process. First, set your measurements. Second, mark out your mat. Third, cut.

At this stage you have already reduced your matboard from the full size sheet and are ready to cut a window in it. Refer to the notes you made earlier, during the design process, for the measurements of the borders you will cut. It's interesting to note that in mat cutting you don't measure and mark out the window of the mat; rather, you measure and mark out the borders that surround the window, and you use the mat guide to do that measuring.

STEP ONE: The mat guide is the narrow metal bar situated in the angled channels beside the guide rail. By loosening the knobs you can slide the mat guide back and forth in the channels and it will always remain parallel to the guide rail (Figure L-1). Beneath the mat guide you will find a scale in $1/16^{th}$ inch increments. Align the mat guide with the size border you want (Figure L-2).

Note: Your mat cutter comes with a backing sheet. This is the long, narrow piece of matboard that lies on the cutting bed

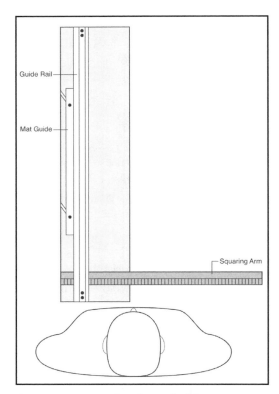

Figure L-3: Stand at the end of the mat cutter.

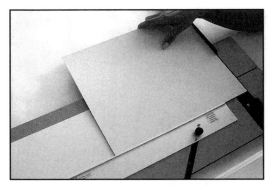

Figure L-4: Place the mat blank against the squaring arm and the mat guide.

Figure L-5: Mark the guide rail.

under the guide rail. Whenever you cut a window, you should use the backing sheet underneath the mat you are cutting. After a while your backing sheet will become well scored and you should replace it. You may use any piece of scrap matboard for this. During sizing, you should remove the backing sheet. It is only for use when cutting a window in a mat.

STEP TWO: Mark out your mat. Stand at the end of the mat cutter (Figure L-3). Lift the guide rail and place the mat face down on the bed of the mat cutter and on top of the backing sheet. If your mat cutter has a squaring arm or squaring bar, bring the bottom edge of the mat into contact with it. Then move the left edge to the left until it rests firmly against the mat guide (Figure L-4). Lower the guide rail.

Using a sharpened pencil, mark a line along the outside edge of the guide rail. Mark the full length of the back of the mat (Figure L-5).

If you are cutting a mat with all four borders the same, turn the mat a quarter turn, replace it under the guide rail with the left edge firmly against the mat guide and mark again. Keep turning the mat and marking until all four borders are marked. If you are cutting a mat with a wider bottom border, mark the first three borders, then readjust the mat guide for the bottom border and mark it.

STEP THREE: Leave the mat in position and put the bevel cutting head onto the

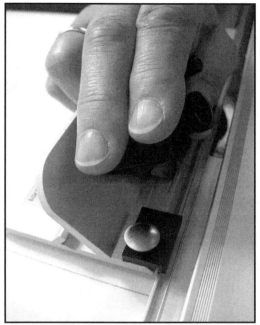

Figure L-6: The plastic guides clip over the outer lip of the guide rail.

Figure L-7: Align the start / stop indicator line with the intersecting pencil line.

of each cutting head will hook easily over the outer lip of the guide rail (Figure L-6). After the cutting head is hooked on, the base of the cutting head should glide along smoothly over the back of the mat.

Locate the start / stop indicator line on the back of the cutting head. Move the cutting head along the guide rail and align the start/stop indicator line with the correct intersecting pencil line (Figure L-7). Which pencil line is correct depends on the model of mat cutter you're using. The Model #750 Simplex Plus Mat Cutter and the Model #450-1 Artist Elite Mat Cutter are operated by pulling toward you as you cut. With these mat cutters, you cut from the top pencil line to the bottom pencil line. The Logan Compact Mat Cutter series is operated by pushing away from you, so you cut from the bottom pencil line to the top pencil line.

Figure L-8: Exert adequate pressure to penetrate the mat.

STEP FOUR: Lower the blade. The depth of the cut has been pre-set by the manufacturer to penetrate standard thickness matboard, so you cannot cut too deeply; you can only fail to cut deeply enough. Exert adequate pressure to penetrate the mat (Figure L-8).

Note: Every Logan mat cutter comes with an adjustable blade depth. On most models this takes the form of a small screw in the base that can be turned in or out to adjust

guide rail. The cutting heads on many Logan models are separate pieces and must be "hooked" onto the guide rail before using. The plastic guides at the front

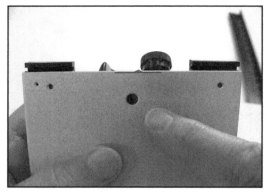

Figure L-9: The cutting head has a blade depth adjustment screw in its base.

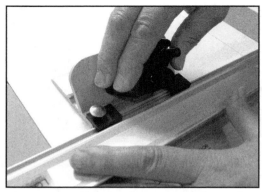

Figure L-10: Cut the mat, applying firm downward pressure on the cutting head as you pull it back.

Figure L-11: By pressing from the back of the mat, you should be able to see that you've cut through the mat.

Figure L-12: The drop-out piece should fall cleanly from the window.

the degree of penetration (Figure L-9). Proper blade depth is crucial to getting good quality cuts and must be readjusted when switching to different thicknesses of matboard.

STEP FIVE: Cut the mat. Apply firm downward pressure on the cutting head as you cut (Figure L-10). Stop your cut when the start/stop indicator line aligns with the opposite intersecting pencil line. Retract the blade from the mat. Remove the cutting head from the guide rail.

STEP SIX: Lift the guide rail. Turn the mat and replace it on the cutting bed on top of the backing sheet. Bring the left edge firmly against the mat guide and the bottom edge firmly against the squaring arm or squaring bar. Lower the guide rail. Hook the cutting head onto the guide rail. Repeat the cutting

procedure. If you are cutting a wider bottom border, you will need to readjust your mat guide after the first cut and reset it to the proper measurement for the remaining borders. When you are finished cutting, the drop-out piece will fall away, revealing the window of your mat.

Note: It is advisable to check your progress as you go. By pressing from the back of the mat, you should be able to see that you've cut completely through (Figure L-11). After you've made two cuts, one corner of the window should be free. After you've made three cuts, the drop-out piece should open like a door. After you've made all four cuts, the drop-out piece should fall cleanly from the window (Figure L-12). If it doesn't, it means you've undercut and you should go back and re-cut—always starting at the beginning and cutting the full length of the cut again. Cut a little bit farther and get the drop-out piece to fall away cleanly, even if it means getting a slight overcut.

Don't be disappointed if your first mat is not perfect. It takes a few tries to become proficient at mat cutting. Even professional framers who have been cutting for years still have trouble from time to time. That's because mat cutting is a skill. It doesn't happen automatically as soon as you buy a mat cutter. To become adept at mat cutting you must anticipate common problems, understand why they occur and know what to do when they occur. A competent framer is a knowledgeable framer.

Troubleshooting

The first step in good mat cutting is to understand common problems and how to deal with them, and among the most common problems in mat cutting are overcuts and undercuts.

Dealing with Overcuts and Undercuts

An overcut is an incision that passes beyond the corner of the mat's window into the face of the mat (Figure M-1). You would think that the manufacturers of mat cutters could design their equipment so the blade would stop precisely on the corner. Yet this is easier said than done. Where the blade starts and stops is due in part to the thickness of the matboard—and matboard varies a great deal in thickness.

Matboard is available in a variety of different cores. The core is the inside

Figure M-1: An overcut is an incision that passes beyond the corner into the face of the mat.

part you see when you bevel cut the mat—bevel cutting refers to cutting the mat at a 45-degree angle. The bevel is the sloped edge that results. Most mats are cut with a beveled edge on the window so the core is quite evident. There is regular cream core matboard, white core rag matboard, regular bleached core matboard, black core matboard, etc. These cores vary in thickness; consequently, there can be a variation in thickness from one type of matboard to another. In addition, the paper that's laminated onto the core can vary in thickness. These face papers give each mat its distinctive color and texture. Consequently, when you change from one color of mat to another, you may encounter a difference in thickness. Bottom line, when you change from one mat to another, it is not unusual to encounter a difference in thickness.

The thickness of the mat affects where the blade starts and stops because as the blade penetrates the mat it moves downward at an angle. Since the mat is typically cut face down, this means the blade enters the back of the mat at a point farther back than it emerges from

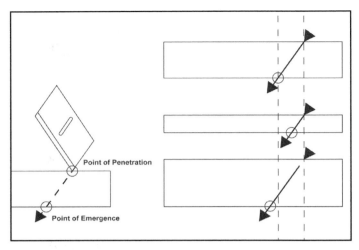

Point of Penetration

Point of Emergence

Figure M-2: The blade enters the back of the mat at a point farther back than it emerges from the face.

the face (Figure M-2).

After cutting your first mat, you may discover that your corner is not perfect, that you have an "overcut". Because the blade moves downward at an angle, it may occur to you to address the problem by adjusting the depth of the cut. This is quite logical.

Since the blade is housed in the mat cutter at an angle, if it is cutting too deeply, it's also extended out too far, meaning that when you get to the end of the cut the blade passes beyond the intersecting cut and gives you an overcut. By adjusting the depth of the cut, it is possible to adjust out the overcut. Fair enough. But eventually you will change to another thickness of mat and the problem will occur again.

Let's say the next mat is marginally thinner than

Figure M-3: To eliminate overcuts and undercuts, move the start and stop indicator line in proper relation to the pencil line.

the mat you cut before. As you cut, the blade penetrates the back of the mat at the same point it did previously, passes through the core at an angle, yet emerges from the face sooner than it did previously—because this mat is thinner. Now you again have an overcut!

If you start with no overcuts and change to a thinner mat, you will get an overcut. If you start with no overcuts and move to a thicker mat, you will get an undercut. Overcuts and undercuts are directly related to the thickness of the matboard and, unfortunately, you're changing thickness of matboard more often than you think. So what are you supposed to do? How do you get a perfect corner?

Start by changing the way you think about mat cutting. The start and stop indicator line that's supposed to tell you where to begin and end each cut cannot be exact because it does not move around on the cutting head to accommodate the different thicknesses of matboard you encounter. Instead, think of the indicator line as a reference, a gauge that can be moved in relation to the pencil lines in order to achieve the results you want (Figure M-3). To eliminate overcuts and undercuts, first diagnose the overcut situation as it exists and then use that information to move the start/stop indicator line in proper relation to the pencil lines.

The easiest way to form a diagnosis is to make some test cuts in the area of your mat that will become the drop-out piece. Mark some lines and cut a test corner there. See what your overcut/undercut situation looks like. Using that information, prepare to cut the actual window but move the start/stop indicator above or below the pencil line by the degree necessary to eliminate the over- or undercut. If you are using a cutting system with production stops instead of a start/stop indicator line, the same problem exists and the same solution is called for, except that with production stops it's a matter of moving the stops on the scales by the degree of the over- or undercut (Figure M-4).

If all of this seems like too much work, there is another method. Go ahead and accept that you will have overcuts and undercuts and then take measures to make them less conspicuous. Most professional picture framers have a tool called a burnishing bone. This is a narrow burnishing tool, sometimes called a bone folder, that looks like a letter opener. By gently rubbing it over an overcut, the overcut is smoothed out, making it less conspicuous (Figure M-5).

If you get an undercut, resist the urge to punch the corner out. Instead, go back to the beginning of the cut, cut the full length of the cut again and cut a little bit farther to get the corner out clean—even at the risk of getting an overcut. As was just mentioned, an overcut can be cleaned up with a burnishing bone, but if you tear the corner by punching it out, you may ruin the mat. If you end up with a small tuft of paper in the corner, you can clean it up with a tool called a mat saver. A mat saver looks suspiciously like a nail file but is somewhat larger and has a heavier grit. A mat saver is commonly used to smooth

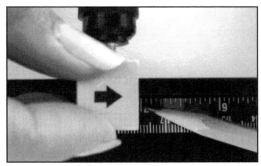

Figure M-4: Move the stop on the scale by the degree of the overcut.

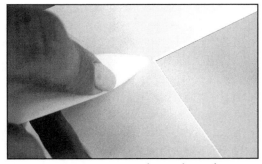

Figure M-5: Use a burnishing bone to smooth down and conceal overcuts.

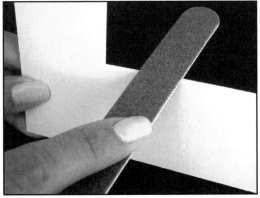

Figure M-6: Use a mat saver to smooth out rough and ragged edges.

out the rough and ragged edges of mats that have been poorly cut (Figure M-6).

Dealing with Rough and Ragged Edges

When you cut a mat, you expect to get clean, sharp edges, but from time to time you get ragged edges. Surprisingly, if you use a backing sheet and are cutting regular matboard, the source of those ragged edges is probably not a dull blade. That's because of what the backing sheet does for you. The backing sheet is there to give you clean cuts. By providing support for the face paper of the mat, the backing sheet prevents the blade from erupting the face paper before breaking through. Because of the added support of the backing sheet, the blade is made to slice rather than punch through the matboard and the result is a clean, sharp edge. If you are using a backing sheet and you encounter a sudden rash of ragged cuts, it's probably not because the blade is dull, but because it's damaged. It's not uncommon for a blade to become chipped or dented, particularly if you forget to retract the blade after cutting. The simple solution is to replace the blade.

Dealing with Inconsistencies in the Beveled Edge

Another common problem in mat cutting is a beveled edge that is not consistent the entire length of the cut. This occurs because the blade flexes and the result is an edge that shows evidence of wavering. To get to the bottom of what causes inconsistency in the angle of the cut, you need to discover what's causing the blade to flex and fix it. There are three general causes of blade flex: First, the mat is not perfectly flat when you cut it; second, something is causing the blade to drag; and third, you may be operating the mat cutter improperly.

To achieve good results in mat cutting, the mat must be flat and firm when you cut it. If the mat is allowed to sag or bow while cutting, the result will be blade flex. First, the mat cutter itself must be on a flat, firm surface. If the table is warped, the entire mat cutter can sag when pressure is applied for

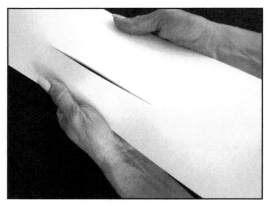

Figure M-7: If the blade cuts too deeply into the backing sheet, you are inviting blade flex.

cutting. As a result, the mat can sag away from the blade, the blade rises in the mat and flexes in response to the change in resistance. Second, there must be no obstruction under the mat during cutting. Even something as seemingly minor as paper scrap or a broken piece of pencil lead can cause trouble. If you are replacing the drop-out piece in the window of the mat (as is necessary when you are double matting), make sure it fits flush within the window. If it's ill-fitted to the window, when the two mats are adhered together, the drop-out piece will be an obstruction and cause the mat to bow slightly.

The second major cause of blade flex is a blade that drags while cutting, and one of the most common causes of drag is a blade that's cutting too deeply. The blade should penetrate the mat and just scratch the surface of the backing sheet. If the blade cuts too deeply or all the way through the backing sheet, you are exposing too much blade, putting excess drag on it and inviting blade flex (Figure M-7). Another common cause of blade drag is a dull blade. As the blade becomes increasingly dull it drags more and more, and as

Figure M-8: Avoid rocking the cutting head. Keep the base of the cutting head flat on the mat.

it drags it flexes. If you encounter a sudden rash of inconsistencies in the beveled edge, replace the blade and, if necessary, adjust the depth of the cut.

When operating the mat cutter, avoid rocking the cutting head (Figure M-8). The cutting head should ride flat on the mat during the entire course of the cut. Also, avoid lateral, or side-to-side, play of the cutting head on the guide rail. Even with a new mat cutter there will be some degree of side-to-side play. Overcome this by using consistent directional pressure down and in throughout the cut (Figure M-9). It's not difficult to see that rocking or wobbling the cutting head can lead to blade flex, and

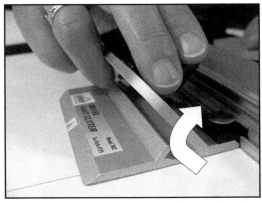

Figure M-9: Overcome side-to-side play by keeping consistent directional pressure down and in throughout the cut.

blade flex in turn can lead to inconsistencies in the beveled edge.

If you can cut a mat with a perfect corner—meaning no evidence of overcuts or undercuts—and one with a clean, sharp beveled edge, and that has a consistent 45-degree edge on its window, you've got a perfect mat. To the extent that good matting is defined by the absence of common problems, being able to recognize and address those problems is crucial to good matting.

Cutting a Double Mat

A double mat is really just two single mats taped together where the window of the mat on top, or "overmat", is slightly larger than the window of the mat underneath, so that the window of the "under mat" appears as a band of color within the window of the overmat. The obvious approach to cutting such a mat would be to cut two mats of the same size where the window of the overmat is slightly larger than the window of the undermat and tape them together. The problem is, the obvious approach doesn't always work.

If the two mat blanks are even slightly out of square, when you try to line them up you will have trouble getting the perimeter edges to line up at the same time you are getting the band of color to line up in the window. Professional picture framers avoid this by trimming the undermat slightly smaller on its perimeter edges, and having done that, they go even further. They employ a technique that allows them to tape the mats together before they make the second set of cuts, and which insures that they will get perfect alignment every time. Here is the technique:

STEP ONE: Cut the window in what will be your overmat. Remember, your overmat will conform to your frame size. Follow the same procedure as you would for cutting a single mat with the following exception: Make the mat borders narrower by the width of the band of color that you want to appear within the window. This band of color is called the "liner" and the finished mat border consists of the overmat plus the liner. Therefore, if your measurements call for mat borders of 2-3⁄4" and you want to have a standard liner of 1⁄4", the border of the overmat will be 2-1⁄2". When you add the 1⁄4" liner, the finished double border will be 2-3⁄4".

STEP TWO: Replace the drop-out piece in the window of the mat you just cut. Lay the drop-out piece face down on a flat surface and place the window mat over it. Fit them together like a puzzle (Figure N-1).

STEP THREE: Cut the mat blank to be used as the undermat. Be sure to make it marginally smaller on its perimeter edges than the overmat. So, if the overmat is 24"x31", the undermat should be about 23-1⁄2"x30-1⁄2", although it doesn't need to be exact.

STEP FOUR: Apply double-sided adhesive transfer tape to the back of the overmat (Figure N-2). The tape most commonly used for this job is ATG tape. ATG tape is a double-sided adhesive transfer tape that fits into a roller applicator gun called an ATG gun. ATG tape can be applied by hand but it is a lot easier to work with in an applicator gun. ATG tape and an ATG gun can be found at most art supply retailers.

STEP FIVE: Affix the undermat face down to the back of the overmat (Figure N-3). Since it is smaller than the overmat, you should be able to position it entirely within the perimeter of the overmat.

STEP SIX: Reset your mat guide in

Figure N-1: Lay the drop-out piece face down and place the window mat over it.

Figure N-2: Apply double-sided adhesive transfer tape to the back of the mat.

Figure N-3: Affix the undermat, which is slightly smaller, face down to the back of the overmat.

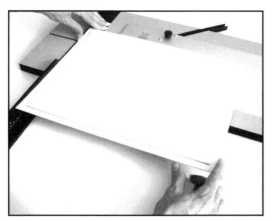

Figure N-4: Place the stack of two mats under the guiderail and firmly against the mat guide.

Figure N-5: Cut the undermat. The result is a perfectly aligned double mat.

preparation for cutting the borders of the finished double mat. Remember, these are the borders that your original measurements called for.

STEP SEVEN: Place your stack of two mats under the guide rail and firmly against the mat guide (Figure N-4).

STEP EIGHT: Lower the guide rail and cut your double mat following the same procedures as you would for a single mat.

The result is a perfectly aligned double mat that is already taped together (Figure N-5). The same procedure can be taken a step further to create a triple mat.

The single mat and double mat are two of the most fundamental matting techniques. But there are others. Read on to learn other essential matting techniques. For additional hints and tips and free streaming video, visit www.LoganGraphic.com.

CHAPTER FIVE

Employing Other Essential Matting Techniques

Once you become comfortable with basic mat cutting, you will probably become more adventurous. Certain questions may arise. How do you cut a mat with more than one window? How do you cut a mat with a round or oval window? How do you cut a decorative accent like a V-groove? What about decorative ink lines? A mat with little steps in each corner? A shadowbox effect? Here are some essential matting techniques to help you expand your matting abilities.

Cutting Multiple Opening Mats

The multiple opening mat, sometimes called a "collage mat", is a mat with a series of windows in it. It is used most often to present photographs.

Much of the challenge in cutting a multiple opening mat is in figuring out the measurements. To simplify the task, you might want to decide on a uniform size for all the windows, even if some photos are larger than others, and try to orient the windows uniformly. In other words, place all the windows in either a portrait orientation or a landscape orientation and avoid mixing them. The more uniform you design your multiple opening mat, the easier it will be to measure and cut.

There are two approaches to determining the placement of the windows in a multiple opening mat. The first is to attack it mathematically beginning with the size and number of the windows and working outward to the frame size. This approach virtually requires that all the windows be uniform, since

using this method to figure out the placement for a variety of different size windows would challenge a Mensa scholar. The second approach is to trace out the size of the windows on some light cardboard, cut them out and arrange them on a sheet of matboard until you are satisfied with their appearance. Then trace around them. This method gives you greater latitude in the sizes and orientation of the windows, but involves a lot of cutting and pasting. In either case, the first step is to determine the size of the windows.

If the windows are to be uniform, they cannot be larger than the smallest photo you have, and should in fact be slightly smaller so the edges of the windows can overlap the edges of the photos and hold them in place. If your smallest photo is 4"x6", the windows should 3-3/4"x5-3/4", providing an eighth-inch overlap along each edge. Now how many windows will you have? Once you've decided on the number of windows, you can then calculate the "bracketing borders" (the outer borders that will surround all the windows).

Let's say you're going to have eight windows of 3-3/4" x 5-3/4" arranged in two rows of four, all in portrait orientation. To calculate the bracketing borders, multiply the width of each window by the number of windows in each row to get the equivalent width of a single window. In our case that would be 3-3/4"x4= 15". Then, multiply the height of each window in each column to get the equivalent height of a single window: 5-3/4" x 2 = 11-1/2". What we discover from this exercise is that if we were going to have a single window rather than eight small windows, that window would be 11-1/2"x15". Referring now to the Border Finder in Chapter One, we find that a single window of 11-1/2"x15" calls for mat borders of 2". Therefore, the bracketing borders for all eight of our small windows should be the same—2".

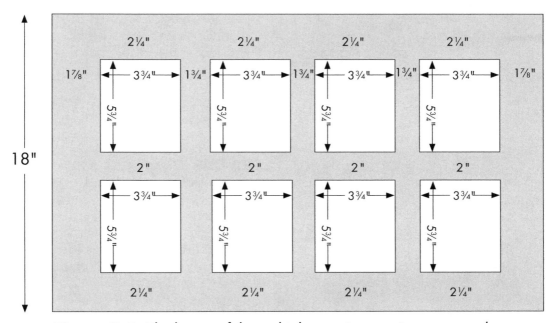

Figure O-1: The layout of the multiple opening mat in our example.

Next, we need to determine how much space should go between each window. The spaces between each window should be no wider than the bracketing borders, but they can be narrower. So we experiment, adding up the spaces, windows and bracketing borders to see what frame size results. If the frame size doesn't suit us, we can modify the spaces or borders. In our case, we have four windows of 3-3/4" and bracketing borders of 2". This takes up 19" of space. There are three spaces between the windows. If the spaces between the windows are the same width as the bracketing borders (2" each), this brings us to a total frame width of 25".

For the height dimension, we have two windows of 5-3/4" with one space between them. If the spaces are the same size as the bracketing borders, this will bring us to a total frame height of 17-1/2".

Looking this over, we see that if we push the height up to 18" and reduce the width to 24", we can fit a standard sized frame of 18"x24". However, we aren't allowed to make the spaces between the windows greater than the bracketing borders. On the other hand, it's all right to make the top and bottom borders marginally wider than the side borders. So if we increase the top and bottom bracketing borders to 2-1/4" and leave the single space between the windows at 2", we arrive at a frame height of 18". To arrive at 24" for the width, we must reduce the frame dimension by an inch. We can do this by reducing the space between each window by 1/4", and then reducing each side border by 1/8". After our modifications, we end up with side borders of 1-7/8"; top and bottom borders of 2-1/4", spaces between the windows on the width dimension of 1-3/4"; and spaces between the windows on the height dimension of 2" (Figure O-1). Now the multiple opening mat will fit into an 18"x24" frame.

Figure O-2: Mark out the windows on your mat blank.

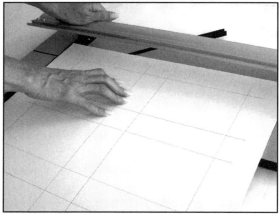

Figure O-3: Place the mat in your cutter and lower the guide rail.

Figure O-4: Align one of the pencil lines defining one of the windows along the guide rail.

Alternatively, you could cut eight 3-3⁄4"x 5-3⁄4" rectangles out of cardboard and arrange them on a mat until they look right and you will probably arrive at about the same conclusion. Two different approaches, same result. Either way, you can see that the most difficult part of cutting a multiple opening mat is designing and measuring it. The cutting is relatively easy.

STEP ONE: Mark out the windows on your mat blank (Figure O-2). Here again a squaring arm comes in handy. With it you can measure and mark a multiple opening mat using your mat cutter. Without it you will have to measure and mark the mat with a rule and straightedge outside your mat cutter.

STEP TWO: Remove the mat guide from your mat cutter, lift the guide rail and place the mat in the cutter (Figure O-3). Lower the guide rail.

STEP THREE: Concentrate on cutting one window at a time. Align one of the pencil lines defining one of the windows along the guide rail (Figure O-4). If you are cutting with a Simplex, Intermediate or Compact mat cutter, always be sure the window is situated to the right of the guide rail as you cut. If the window is ever to the left of the guide rail, you will end up with a "reverse bevel", a bevel that slopes outward toward the back of the mat and is not visible from the face. A reverse bevel will ruin the mat, requiring you to start over again.

STEP FOUR: Cut one window at a time. Cut all four sides of the window and the drop-out piece will fall away.

STEP FIVE: Repeat the procedure for the remaining windows, focusing on proper placement of each window rela-

Figure O-5: The finished multiple opening mat will result.

tive to the guide rail before cutting. The finished multiple-opening mat will result (Figure O-5).

Cutting Oval and Circle Mats

Logan makes a mat cutter designed especially to cut oval and circle mats. The Model #201 Oval and Circle Mat Cutter operates independently of any other mat cutter and cuts ovals from 3"x 4-1/2" up to 20"x23" and circles from 4" to 20". As with most mat cutters, there is a learning curve associated with it. The following step-by-step procedure will provide deeper insights to help you to shorten the learning curve and begin producing quality oval and circle mats faster.

STEP ONE: Set the shape of the oval or circle. The design of the Model #201 Oval and Circle Mat Cutter has a bevel cutting head mounted to an arm that rotates around a stationary base. A cam-shaped plate with an adjustable mid-point allows for the setting of different ellipses (Figure P-1). Each shape is determined by adjusting the scale inside the base for the difference between the height and width of the window you want to cut. For example, if you want to cut an 8"x 10" oval, you set the differential scale to 2", because 2 is the difference between 8 and 10. If you want a shorter, squatter oval, an 8"x9" is called for and the differ-

ential scale is set at 1. By changing the difference between the height and the width, you change the shape of the oval. By setting the difference between the height and width to zero, you are setting up to cut a circle.

STEP TWO: On the rotating arm, you will find a separate scale. Slide the cutting head along this arm and lock it down at the point on the scale indicative of the narrow dimension of your oval (Figure P-2). For example, if you want to cut an 8"x 10", set the scale on the arm to 8". When the differential scale is set to zero, the setting

Figure P-1: A cam-shaped plate with an adjustable mid-point allows for the setting of different ellipses.

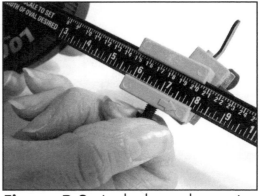

Figure P-2: Lock down the cutting head at the point equal to the narrow dimension of the oval you want to cut.

on the scale arm indicates the diameter of the circle you will cut.

STEP THREE: Position the oval cutter on the mat. On the front of the mat mark a large plus sign (larger than the base) where you want the middle of the oval window to be (Figure P-3). Note: Unlike other mat cutters, oval and circle mat cutters are designed to cut on the front of the mat.

STEP FOUR: Anchor the base to the mat. First, place a second mat of the same size under the mat you are going to cut. This second mat is the backing sheet.

Without it you will cut through your mat and into the table top. Next, arrange the base over the plus sign, aligning the pointers on each side of the base with the arms of the plus sign (Figure P-4). Caution: The base must be oriented to the mat the same way you want the window oriented to the mat. For example, in most cases you don't want a horizontal oval oriented to the vertical axis of the mat.

STEP FIVE: Press down firmly on the base with the heels of your hands (Figure P-5). The pins under the base will sink into the mat helping to anchor it. However, the pins will not be enough to hold the base in place once you begin cutting. During cutting you must always hold down firmly on the base with one hand.

STEP SIX: Allow the cutting head to swivel into the starting position. The cutting head is

Figure P-3: On the front of the mat mark a large plus sign (larger than the base) where you want the middle of the oval to be.

Figure P-4: Align the pointers on each side of the base with the arms of the plus sign.

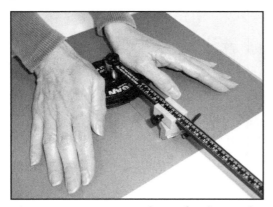

Figure P-5: Press down firmly on the base with the heels of your hands.

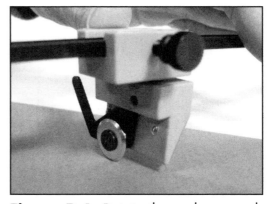

Figure P-6: Rotate the scale arm, allowing the cutting head to swivel into the starting position.

mounted on a pin under the scale arm and is designed to swivel (Figure P-6). Without the ability to swivel it would be impossible to cut different shaped ovals. Before engaging the blade, it's necessary to allow the cutting head to swivel into position. Holding down firmly on the cutting head, rotate the scale

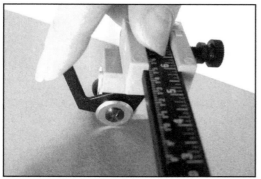

Figure P-7: With your thumb resting on top of the cutting head, lift the stepping lever until it clicks into the first step.

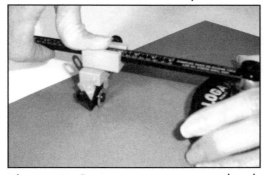

Figure P-8: As you cut, rest your thumb lightly on top of the cutting head but keep your fingers out of its way.

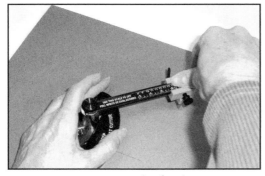

Figure P-9: During the final rotations exert moderate downward pressure with your thumb on top of the cutting head.

arm around the base. Do not engage the blade. The cutting head will roll forward on its tracking wheel and swivel to assume the curvature of the oval. Caution: The scale arm must only be rotated around the base in a clockwise direction. Caution: Do not allow your fingers to touch or obstruct the swiveling cutting head, doing so will prevent the cutting head from swiveling into position and will result in a frayed cut.

STEP SEVEN: Engage the blade. With your thumb resting lightly on top of the cutting head, lift the stepping lever until it clicks into the first step. You will feel it click in. The blade is now engaged (Figure P-7). Caution: You are now at the most critical stage in the procedure. Anything you do to block or obstruct the swiveling cutting head will result in a frayed cut. Do not let your fingers touch the swiveling cutting head as you rotate the scale arm. However, to achieve the best results, rest your thumb lightly on top of the cutting head (Figure P-8).

STEP EIGHT: Rotate the scale arm around the base, making a light initial score in the surface of the mat. The cutter is not designed to cut through at this point. Do not exert downward pressure with your thumb on top of the cutting head; simply let it rest lightly there as you rotate the arm. Keep your fingers well out of the way of the swiveling cutting head. Rotate past the point where the score joins itself.

STEP NINE: With your thumb resting lightly on top of the cutting head, reach down with your index finger and lift the stepping lever to the next step. Rotate the scale arm around the base again. You will feel an increase in resistance as the blade cuts more deeply into the mat. Rotate past the point where you started the cut.

STEP TEN: Lift the stepping lever to the final step. Rotate the scale arm around the base two or three more times. You cannot cut too many times; you can only fail to cut enough times to penetrate the mat. During the final rotations you can exert moderate downward pressure with your thumb on top of the cutting head to insure cutting through (Figure P-9).

Figure P-10: Lift away the drop-out piece.

STEP ELEVEN: Disengage the blade and lift away the drop-out piece (Figure P-10). Your oval is complete.

The procedure is exactly the same for cutting circles. The only difference is in how you set up the cutter.

Cutting V-Groove Mats

The Logan Models #703, #705 and #706 V-Groove Cutters are designed to carve decorative V-shaped grooves in the surface of a mat. The Model #703 is for use with Model #750 Simplex Plus Mat Cutter, as well as with the Model #450 Intermediate Mat Cutter and the Compact Mat Cutters with the addition of a Model #303 Adapter. The Model #705 is for use with the Logan #650 Framer's Edge Mat Cutter. The Model #706 is for use with other brands of mat cutters.

V-grooves are delicate, low-key accents used to offset artwork and direct the viewer's eye into the composition. For best effect they are placed about a quarter of the way inside the mat border from the edge of the mat window. The V-groove cutter works by engaging two 45-degree opposing blades in succession, first by pushing away, then by pulling toward you. The first blade cuts marginally farther than the second, creating a mitered corner. The cutter begins and ends each cut with a stop.

Step One: Before you attempt to cut a V-groove with the Logan V-Groove Cutter it's necessary to make delicate calibrations or adjustments to the stops and the cutter. A piece of scrap matboard should be used to make test cuts while adjusting. Adjust the width of the V-groove by loosening the red knob and moving the two blade holders closer together or further apart (Figure Q-1). Adjust the eccentric post on top of the mat cutter. This post comes into contact with the top stop and creates your stopping point when pushing the cutter away from you (Figure Q-2). Finally, adjust the screw seated in the rear guide. This screw comes into contact with the bottom stop and creates your

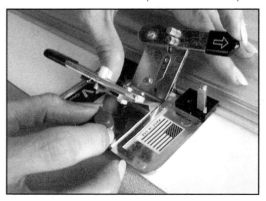

Figure Q-1: Adjust the width of the V-groove by loosening the red knob and moving the two blade holders in relation to each other.

Figure Q-2: To adjust the stopping point of the mat cutter, adjust the eccentric post.

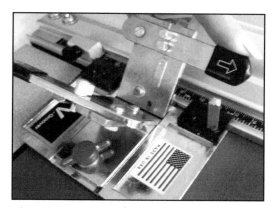

Figure Q-3: To begin the cut, bring the V-Groover into contact with the bottom stop and lower the lever with the arrow pointing away from you.

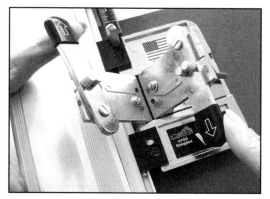

Figure Q-4: When the V-Groover comes into contact with the top stop, retract the blade and lower the opposing blade.

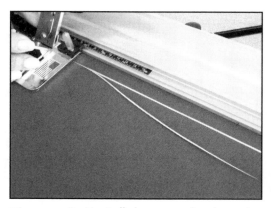

Figure Q-5: Pull the cutter back until it again contacts the bottom stop.

stopping point when pulling toward you.

Step Two: It's best to cut the V-grooves before you cut the window in the mat. Set your stops and place the V-groove cutter on the guide rail. Bring it into contact with the bottom stop. Lower the lever with the arrow pointing away from you (Figure Q-3). Push the cutter away from you.

Step Three: When the V-Groove Cutter comes into contact with the top stop, retract the blade and lower the opposing blade (Figure Q-4). Caution: Make sure the first blade is fully retracted before lowering the opposing blade. Failure to do so may cause the blades to scrape together, dulling them and leading to a gritty V-groove.

Step Four: Pull the cutter back until it again contacts the bottom stop (Figure Q-5). Retract the blade.

Step Five: Repeat the procedure for the remaining three sides. When your V-groove is complete, cut the window in the mat. You now have a mat with a decorative V-groove in it (Figure Q-6).

Putting Decorative Ink Lines on Your Mat

Matting techniques such as V-grooves or ink lines are distinguished from other types

Figure Q-6: A decorative V-groove results.

of creative matting in that they involve enhancements to the surface of the mat rather than variations in the window itself. They serve as launching points for even greater elaboration. Decorative ink lines, for instance, are the basis for painted panels that involve coloring between the lines with watercolors or pastels. The traditional French mat with its elegant combination of lines and washes is really just an elaboration of basic ink lines. So competence with a range of surface designs requires, first, a mastery of decorative ink lines.

The application of ink lines requires the use of a ruling pen and a straightedge. Most professional framers use a quality dual-nib inking pen for this purpose because the nibs can be adjusted to produce different thicknesses of lines and because the ink is permanent and non-fading. However, for casual work you can get by with an inexpensive fine-point felt-tip pen. The guide rail of your mat cutter can serve as your straightedge for this purpose.

Apply the ink lines before cutting the window in the mat. For best effect, place them about a quarter of the way inside the mat border from the edge of the mat's window. The ink lines will be drawn between tick marks that you place on the surface of the mat. Precise placement of the tick marks is essential. A tool called a corner marker can make this part of the procedure easier.

STEP ONE: Place tick marks on the face of your mat. Measure down from the top edge of the matboard and in from the left edge, locating the point at which you want to begin your first line. Using a pencil, make a small, light tick mark (Figure R-1). Turn the mat a quarter turn and repeat the procedure, placing the tick mark for the end of your first line and the beginning

of your second. Keep turning the mat until all four tick marks are down.

STEP TWO: The real trick when applying ink lines is to avoid the blotching that occurs when the pen first contacts or leaves the mat. Magic Tape™ by 3M provides the solution. Place a small tab of Magic Tape™ just below the bottom tick mark. Place it as close as possible to the tick mark. In fact, place the tape so it is against the tick mark (Figure R-2). Place a second tab of Magic Tape™ above and against the top tick mark.

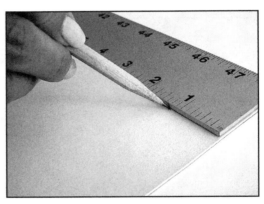

Figure R-1: Measure down from the top edge of the matboard and in from the left edge, locating the point at which you want to begin your first line. Make a tick mark.

Figure R-2: Place a small tab of removable tape just below the bottom tick mark.

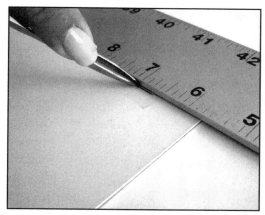

Figure R-3: Start drawing the line on the tape.

Figure R-4: Move the pen along the guide rail at constant speed. Stop the line on the bottom tab of tape.

STEP THREE: Position the mat under the guide rail of your mat cutter and align the outside edge of the guide rail with the tick marks.

STEP FOUR: Draw the first line. Start drawing the line on the tape (Figure R-3). The pen will already be moving forward when it contacts the mat. Move the pen along the guide rail at a constant speed (Figure R-4). Stop drawing the line on the tape at the opposite end. By starting and stopping each line on the tape, any blotching that occurs will occur on the tape.

STEP FIVE: Lift the guide rail and peel up the tape (Figure R-5). Your line begins and ends crisply and precisely at each end.

STEP SIX: Repeat the procedure for the remaining three sides, endeavoring to begin and end each line in exact conjunction with the adjoining lines. Erase the tick marks. Cut the window in the mat. Decorative ink lines nicely enhance the window of your mat (Figure R-6).

Cutting Stepped Corner Mats

Placing two small steps at each corner of a mat's window creates an elegant effect reminiscent of an art deco motif. The cutting

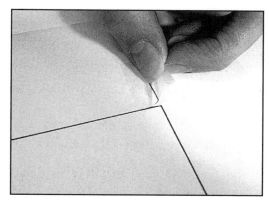

Figure R-5: Lift the guide rail and peel up the tape.

Figure R-6: Decorative ink lines enhance the window of your mat.

part of the procedure is relatively simple once you've gotten the procedure straight in your mind. But getting the procedure straight can be somewhat challenging.

To begin with, realize that in most cases when cutting a mat, you begin and end each cut on the same set of pencil lines. This is because you have only one set of pencil lines to work with. However, when you cut a stepped corner mat, you have three sets of pencil lines to work with. You will not always start and stop on the same set of lines. In fact, to cut steps in the corners of a mat, you must start and stop on the set of lines opposite those you're cutting whenever possible. (In this case, by "opposite" we mean as in outermost versus innermost.)

STEP ONE: Mark your lines. You will mark your first set of lines a half inch outside the border width your measurements called for. So, if your measurements called for 2" borders, draw your first set of lines at 2-1/2". Then reset your mat guide and draw your next set of lines a quarter inch inside the first. In our example, the next set of lines would be at 2-1/4". Reset your mat guide for the border width called for in your measurements and draw a third set of lines. In our case, the setting would be 2".

STEP TWO: You now have three sets of lines, each inside of the next—three marked out rectangles, as it were. The largest of the three surrounds the other two and will henceforth be referred to as the outermost rectangle. The smallest of the three is surrounded by the other two and will be referred to as the innermost rectangle. The rectangle lying between them is the middle rectangle.

STEP THREE: Leave the mat guide where

it was set when you drew your last set of lines. Place the mat in the mat cutter face down under the guide rail and firmly against the mat guide. Bring the bevel cutting head into position to start your cut. You will be confronted with three lines at the start of the cut. The question of which line to start on is most pertinent to the success of this technique. Remember, where possible you will always start and stop the cut on the set of pencil lines opposite the ones you are cutting. So which set of lines are you cutting? Whichever rectangle is lined up against the guide rail is the rectangle you are cutting. If you didn't move your mat guide since drawing your last line, the rectangle you are cutting first will be the outermost rectangle. So you will start and stop each cut on the set of lines that make up the innermost rectangle (which is opposite the outermost).

STEP FOUR: Align the start and stop indicator line on your cutting head with the top of the innermost rectangle (Figure S-1). Cut until you reach the bottom of the inner-

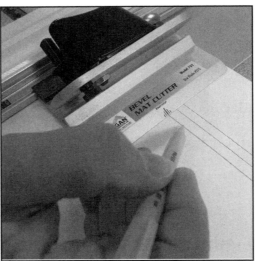

Figure S-1: Align the start and stop indicator line with the top of the innermost rectangle.

most rectangle (Figure S-2). Cut all four sides starting and stopping on the lines that make up the innermost rectangle. At this point your cuts will not meet in the corners.

Figure S-2: Cut until you reach the bottom of the innermost rectangle.

Figure S-3: Align the start and stop indicator with the top of the middle rectangle.

Figure S-4: Cut until you reach the bottom of the middle rectangle.

STEP FIVE: Readjust the mat guide to cut the middle rectangle, a quarter inch wider than the setting you were just at. In our example, the setting will be 2-1/4". Now the middle rectangle will be aligned against the guide rail. Since there is no rectangle opposite to the middle line, you will start and stop this cut on the middle rectangle. Align the start/stop indicator line with the top of the middle rectangle (Figure S-3). Cut until you reach the bottom of the middle rectangle (Figure S-4). Cut all four lines starting and stopping on the middle rectangle. After this set of cuts the drop-out piece will fall from the window.

STEP SIX: Readjust the mat guide a quarter inch wider than the last setting, taking it back to the setting it was at when you drew the first set of lines. In our case, that setting is 2-1/2". For the remaining four cuts you will have to hold the drop-out piece in the window. Fit the drop-out piece back into the window and, holding it together, replace the mat under the guide rail (Figure S-5).

STEP SEVEN: Now the innermost rectangle will be aligned against the guide rail. So you will start and stop your cuts on the outermost rectangle. Align the start/stop

Figure S-5: Fit the drop-out piece back into the window and replace the mat in the cutter.

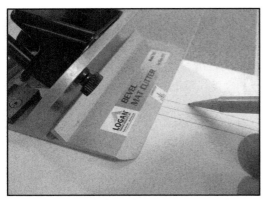

Figure S-6: Align the start/stop indicator line with the top of the outermost rectangle.

Figure S-7: Cut until you reach the bottom of the outermost rectangle.

Figure S-8: The drop-out piece and long strips fall away, revealing the stepped corner mat.

indicator line with the top of the outermost rectangle (Figure S-6). Cut until you reach the bottom of the outermost rectangle (Figure S-7). Caution: As you cut, long strips will fall from the mat. Remove these as they fall out so they don't become an obstruction. Caution: As the strips fall away, the window will become larger; however, the drop-out piece will remain the same size.

Soon the drop-out piece will slide and shift in the window space. Let it. You still need the drop-out piece in place to keep the bevel cutting head riding on a level plane. Caution: By this stage in the process it becomes difficult to keep clear which side you've cut and which side you haven't. It's easy to get confused and cut the same side twice. To avoid this, turn the mat a quarter turn clockwise after each cut. This way, if you get lost, you can stay on track simply by turning the mat clockwise after each cut and counting out four cuts.

STEP EIGHT: After you've cut your final set of cuts, the long strips and the drop-out piece fall away, revealing a stepped corner mat (Figure S-8).

Creating Shadow Box Effects

Occasionally for aesthetic effect framers want to raise the window mat off the artwork so it appears to be suspended above the artwork, sort of hovering there. This is called a shadow box effect. There is some confusion with this terminology since "shadow box" also refers to the type of deep frame used for displaying three-dimensional objects, also known as an object box. What we're talking about here is a shadow box effect.

The shadow box effect works best when the artwork is displayed as a matted float. As a reminder, a matted float involves first mounting the artwork on a mat blank and then cutting a window in the mat that's larger than the artwork, revealing the edges of the artwork and a margin of the mat blank within the window. Selecting the color of the mat blank, then, is much like selecting the color of the undermat in a double mat. It is an accent color which surrounds the artwork in a narrow band. In the case of a shadowbox effect, the accent color does not end abruptly at the edge of the mat's window but fades into the shadowy recesses under the mat which is raised above it. The technique for float mounting the artwork to the mat blank will be covered in the next chapter. Here we will concern ourselves with raising the window mat above the mat blank, a procedure accomplished with the use of foamboard.

STEP ONE: Using a 90-degree cutting head adjusted to its lowest depth setting, cut a sheet of 1/8" thick foamboard into narrow strips (Figure T-1). The length and width of those strips depends on the size of your mat and the width of its borders. The strips should always be slightly narrower than half the width of the border. So if the mat border is 2", the strip should be about 7/8" wide.

You don't have to be exact. The main objective is to conceal the strips under the mat's borders so they can't be seen when the mat is viewed from the side. The length of the first two strips should be slightly less than the length of the mat. Again, you don't have to be exact. If the length of the mat is 20", the first two strips can be 19". The length of the remaining two strips must take into account the presence of the first two strips. They should be shorter than the mat is wide, minus the width of the other two strips. So if, say, the mat is 16" wide and the other two strips are 7/8" wide, strips of 13-1/2" ought to suffice (Figure T-2).

STEP TWO: Apply double-sided adhesive tape or ATG tape to both sides of each strip (Figure T-3).

Figure T-2: The length of the remaining two strips must fit within the other two strips already in place.

Figure T-1: Cut a sheet of 1/8" thick foamboard into narrow strips.

Figure T-3: Apply double-sided adhesive tape on both sides of each strip.

Figure T-4: With the artwork already affixed to the mat blank, assemble the strips beside each edge of the mat blank.

Figure T-5: Place the window mat down against the strips.

STEP THREE: With the artwork already affixed to the mat blank, assemble the strips on the mat blank, bringing them close to, but not against, the edges of the blank (Figure T-4).

STEP FOUR: Place the window mat down against the strips of foamboard, adhering it to them (Figure T-5). Your shadowbox effect is now complete.

CHAPTER SIX

Mounting Your Artwork

"Mounting" your artwork is just a fancy way of saying that you will be attaching your artwork for presentation within a mat window or against a mat blank or backing board. There are three basic methods for mounting artwork. You can attach it by coating it with adhesive. You can suspend it using tabs of tape. Or you can trap it along its edges or at its corners. Within each method a variety of techniques exist. Which technique you use depends on the type of presentation you want to make and the value of the artwork. If the artwork has a great deal of potential value, you will want to limit your mounting materials and techniques to those that are of archival quality.

Grappling with Conservation and Archival Concerns

In a typical conservation or archival frame job, the main objective is keep acid-bearing materials out of direct contact with the artwork. Untreated acid-bearing materials can seep acid which, when in contact with artwork, leaves a brown hazy effect called acid burn. Acid burn is a stain that permanently damages and devalues artwork. Materials used in conservation and archival framing are acid free for the express purpose of safeguarding artwork so it retains its value.

It stands to reason, therefore, that any mounting technique that might cause artwork to lose its value would also be off the table. Bearing this in mind, the process of coating a piece of artwork with adhesive and permanently sticking it down would not be considered archival, since sticking anything permanently to anything else tends to devalue it. For this reason the first method of mounting, called permanent mounting, should only be used for artwork unlikely to increase in value over time.

Permanent Mounting

Dry mounting involves a tissue impregnated with adhesive placed between the artwork and the mounting board, which is usually foamboard. With the application of heat the adhesive melts, creating a uniform coat of adhesive between the artwork and the mounting board. With the use of a steel platen or vacuum, the artwork is pressed uniformly against the mounting board. The resulting mount is flat, firm and uniform with no sign of buckles or waves. Dry mounting is such an effective technique that it is a favorite of many professionals, but the high cost of dry-mount presses makes it impractical for most novices.

Do-it-yourself picture framers often fall back on spray mounting as an accessible option. Spray mounting involves coating the back of the artwork with an aerosol adhesive. Performed properly, the work area is covered liberally with newspaper and the artwork is placed face down on it. The adhesive is sprayed from 8 to 12 inches away in a sweeping motion traveling across the plane of the artwork and out onto the surrounding newspaper (Figure U-1). The work area should be well ventilated and the user should wear a paper respirator mask. Spray adhesives can be unpleasantly messy and one has to be careful to avoid adhesives that are not repositionable. If it is not the repositionable type, your artwork will stick permanently to the mounting board the moment it contacts the adhesive, and if you don't position the artwork perfectly to begin with, your artwork will be ruined.

Less messy and unforgiving are permanent mounting boards. These four-ply paper boards have the rigidity of illustration board and are coated with an adhesive that only becomes permanent once you burnish it. Peel back the release paper and place the artwork face up on the mounting board (Figure U-2). Position the release paper over the artwork and burnish through it, adhering the artwork to the mounting board (Figure U-3). Because the unmounted portion of the board is not presentable, it must be covered with a mat, making it impractical for float mounting.

For the do-it-yourselfer the preferred method is Positionable Mounting Adhesive or PMA. PMA is a more versatile technique than permanent mounting boards because it can be used for float mounting. In addition, it is cleaner and safer than spray mounting and much less expensive than dry mounting. Although a machine can be purchased for applying it, PMA can be applied manually with relative ease.

PMA is a 50-foot sheet of transferable adhesive on a roll. The rolls are available in 11", 16" and 24" widths. For larger artwork, two swatches of PMA can be applied side-by-side with a slight overlap. No evidence of a seam will be visible. The package also contains release paper, a plastic burnishing squeegee and instructions.

Step One: Unroll a length of PMA larger than the item you are mounting and cut it

Figure U-1: With spray mounting, the adhesive is sprayed from 8 to 12 inches away in a sweeping motion.

Figure U-2: With permanent mounting boards, peel back the release paper and place the artwork face up on the board.

Figure U-3: Position release paper over the artwork and burnish through it.

with a razor blade (Figure U-4).

Step Two: Place the artwork face up on the tacky side of the sheet (Figure U-5).

Step Three: Place the release paper over the artwork and burnish through it, transferring the adhesive from the sheet onto the back of the artwork (Figure U-6).

Step Four: Peel the artwork away from the sheet. The adhesive should transfer from the sheet to the back of the artwork in a uniform coat (Figure U-7).

Step Five: Position the artwork on foamboard or a mat blank (if you want to float mount it). If you are unhappy with the positioning, peel up the artwork and try again. The artwork will peel up cleanly because PMA is fully re-

positionable until you burnish it a second time. Once you are satisfied, place the release paper over the artwork and burnish it again to adhere it permanently (Figure U-8).

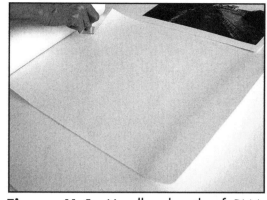

Figure U-4: Unroll a length of PMA larger than the item you are mounting and cut it with a razor blade.

Figure U-5: Place the artwork face up on the tacky side of the sheet.

Figure U-6: Place the release paper over the artwork and burnish through it.

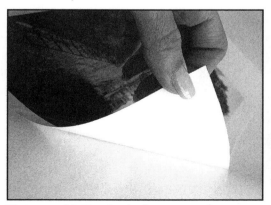

Figure U-7: Peel the artwork away from the sheet.

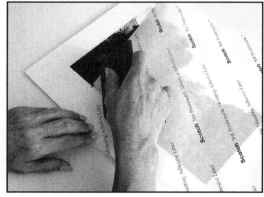

Figure U-8: Arrange the artwork on the mat blank or mounting board and burnish it down.

Hinge Mounting

"Hinge mounting" is framer-speak for mounting artwork by suspending it with tabs of tape. When performed using tapes designed for the purpose, hinge mounting is considered a sound archival mounting method and can be used with one-of-a-kind artwork, such as original art on paper or limited-edition prints. Proper hinging tapes are acid free and have the quality of "reversibility", meaning that the stickiness of the adhesive can be reversed and the tape can be peeled cleanly off the artwork without damaging it, if need be.

T-Hinge

The most common hinge mounting method is called the T-hinge. It is used when the window of the mat is slightly smaller than the artwork and the edges of the mat's window overlap the edges of the paper. A tab of tape is applied vertically at the top edge of the artwork about two inches from the corner (Figure V-1). Half the tape is adhered to the back of the artwork and half to the back of the mat. A second tab of tape is applied vertically in the same manner about two inches from the opposite corner. Then both tabs of tape are crossed with additional tabs of tape for the purpose of reinforcing the hold of the first tabs against the back of the mat (Figure V-2).

Note: Only two tabs of tape are employed against the artwork. The artwork is not taped along the full length of the top edge, nor is it taped at the sides or the bottom. It simply hangs in the window. The reason for this is two-fold. First, you want to conserve the artwork; you want to minimize the amount of adhesive you put into contact with it. Second, it is the nature of paper that it "breathes". That is, it expands and contracts as it absorbs and releases moisture. Unless you are

going to coat the paper with adhesive (as with dry mounting or PMA), you cannot prevent it from breathing, and anything you do to restrict it from breathing will create buckles and waves. In fact, most artwork that shows evidence of buckles and waves has been improperly mounted by taping it along the full length of the top edge or at the sides or bottom. Proper hinge mounting promotes breathing by taping the artwork at only two points.

V-Hinge

When the mat is out of contact with the artwork,

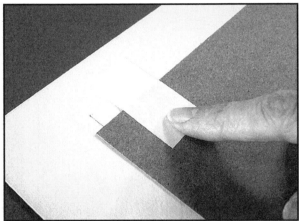

Figure V-1: A tab of tape is applied vertically at the top edge of the artwork about two inches in from the corner.

Figure V-2: Both tabs of tape are crossed horizontally with additional tabs of tape for reinforcement.

as is the case with a matted float or shadow box effect, the T-hinge is not an option, so you must mount to the mounting board or mat blank using a method called the V-hinge.

STEP ONE: Place the artwork on the mounting board and place the window mat over it. Arrange the artwork in the window of the mat, then remove the window mat. The artwork should be lying on the mounting board correctly positioned. Using a straightedge, mark guide lines at the corners of the artwork so you can remove it and replace it in the proper position (Figure V-3). Mark the full length of the top of the artwork.

STEP TWO: Keeping the top edge of the artwork lined up with guideline, turn it over (Figure V-4). Apply a tab of tape vertically about two inches from the corner so that half the tape is on the back of the artwork and half is on the mounting board (Figure V-5). Apply a second tab of tape in the same manner about two inches from the opposite corner. Then cross each tab of tape with a second tab of tape applied horizontally. This second tab of tape doesn't touch the artwork but serves to reinforce the hold of the first tab against the mounting board and provides an operable hinge point.

STEP THREE: Turn the artwork back over again, concealing the tape (Figure V-6). Place your mat over the artwork.

Figure V-3: Using a straightedge, mark guidelines along the top edge and at the corners of the artwork.

Figure V-4: Keeping the artwork aligned with the guideline along the top edge, flip it over.

Figure V-5: Apply a tab of tape vertically about two inches from the corner.

Figure V-6: Flip the artwork back over again, concealing the tape.

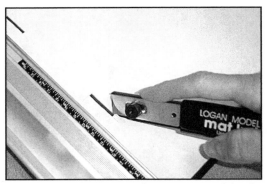

Figure V-7: Cut a slot in a mat blank using a Logan Mat Knife.

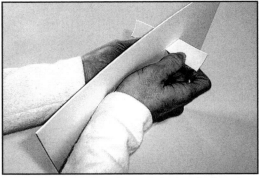

Figure V-8: Feed tape through the slot.

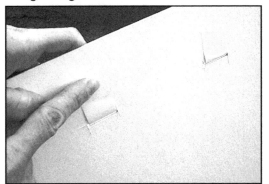

Figure V-9: Adhere tape to the back of the mat in the area above the slot.

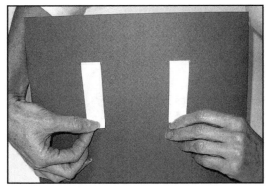

Figure V-10: Pull the tape taut down the face.

S-Hinge

Sometimes heavy artwork, such as heavy watercolor paper, may pull against the tabs of a V-hinge, in time exposing them in a float mount presentation. Or you may have loose media like pastels or charcoals which cannot tolerate being flipped over onto their faces to be worked with. In these cases, you will employ the S-hinge. The S-hinge always involves a mat blank, which will subsequently be backed by foamboard. Begin by cutting narrow slits in the mat blank.

STEP ONE: To find the location for the slits, turn the mat blank upside down and place the artwork on the back of it, position it where it will be when mounted on the face. Mark some guide lines to indicate this position. Then remove the artwork. About an inch down from where the top edge of the artwork will be located and about two inches

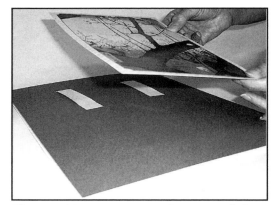

Figure V-11: Position the artwork face up on the tape.

from where the left edge will be, cut a slit in the matboard using a Logan Mat Knife (Figure V-7). Repeat for a second slit two inches from where the right edge will be. Caution: Don't attempt to cut through the mat in one pass; instead, score four to six times to get a relatively clean cut. You will be feeding tape through these slits so make them wide enough to accommodate the tape.

STEP TWO: Cut two tabs of tape about four to six inches long and feed them through the slits. The tape should be adhesive side out as it hangs down the face of the mat (Figure V-8).

STEP THREE: Adhere the tape to the back of the mat in the area above the slit (Figure V-9).

STEP FOUR: On the face of the mat, pull the tape taut and tape it down with a second tab of tape to prevent curling (Figure V-10).

STEP FIVE: Position the artwork face up on the tape (Figure V-11).

Trapping Methods

If we acknowledge that using a minimal amount of adhesive on artwork helps to conserve it, then using no adhesive must be an even better approach. The trapping methods do just that. By cradling artwork, trapping ensures the ability to recover artwork in exactly the same condition as the day it was framed.

Perhaps the simplest trapping method is to use a product called See-Thru Archival Mounting Strips by Lineco, Inc. (Lineco makes many of the mounting and hinging tapes used in picture framing.) An Archival

Mounting Strip is a clear Mylar flange with a band of adhesive along one edge. The adhesive holds the strip to the mat while the Mylar flange overlaps and traps the artwork. Position your artwork on the mounting board. Peel the release paper from the adhesive band (Figure W-1) and place the strip along one edge of the artwork (Figure W-2). Trap the artwork at each edge and then cover it with your window mat (Figure W-3).

A variation on the same idea are adhesive mounting corners, called Photo Corners or Framer's Corners. Here you trap the artwork in triangular pockets at each corner. (Think in terms of an old time photo album.) Position the artwork on the mounting board. Mark

Figure W-1: Peel the release paper from the adhesive band.

Figure W-2: Assemble a strip along each edge of the artwork.

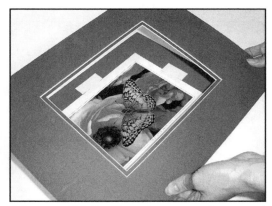

Figure W-3: Trap the artwork at each edge, then cover it with your window mat.

lines on the mounting board to indicate the position of the corners. Peel the corners from the release paper (Figure W-4) and stick them down. Fit the corners of the artwork into

Figure W-4: Peel a corner from the release paper.

Figure W-5: Fit the corners of the artwork into the pockets.

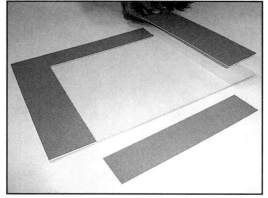

Figure W-6: Affix the strips to the face of the mounting board.

the pockets (Figure W-5) and your artwork is mounted.

When it comes to heavy watercolor paper, canvas boards or other relatively flat yet heavy items, including magazines, books and record albums, the best approach may well be the sink mount. A sink mount is made by affixing strips of matboard or foamboard to the surface of a mounting board, creating a shallow recess or "sink" into which the artwork is placed. When covered by a window mat, the artwork is trapped front-to-back as well as side-to-side.

The thickness of the strip material should be about the same thickness as the item you are framing. If you are mounting a thick magazine or book, for example, foamboard would be called for; if you are mounting a canvas board, matboard would be your best bet; and if you are mounting heavy watercolor paper, you might want to make your strips out of a second piece of heavy watercolor paper.

To create a sink mount, measure the artwork. Then figure out the height and width of the strips you will need to create the sink.

STEP ONE: To figure the height of the strips to be placed along the top and bottom of the mounting board, subtract the height of the artwork from the height of the frame and divide the difference in half. The width of these strips will be the same as the width of the mounting board.

STEP TWO: To figure the width of the strips to be placed along the sides, subtract the width of the artwork from the width of the frame and divide the difference in half. The height of these strips is the height of the mounting board minus the height of the top and bottom strips.

STEP THREE: Using a 90-degree cutting head, cut the strips from a larger sheet.

STEP FOUR: Apply double-sided adhesive tape or ATG tape to each strip and affix them to the face of the mounting board (Figure W-6). Place each strip flush with the edge of

Figure W-7: Place your artwork in the sink, trapping it side-to-side and top-to-bottom.

Figure W-8: Place your window mat over the sink.

the mounting board. When the strips are in place, you will have created a recess on the surface of the mat—a sink.

STEP FIVE: Place your artwork in the sink, trapping it side-to-side and top-to-bottom (Figure W-7).

STEP SIX: Place your window mat over the sink (Figure W-8). The edges of the mat's window will overlap the edges of the artwork, trapping it front-to-back. If you wish, you can also affix the window mat to the sink with double-sided tape.

Mounting Stretched Canvas

Because there is no mat or glass involved in framing stretched canvas, it is among the easiest items to frame. However, canvas stretched on stretcher bars is often thicker than the depth of the frame you're putting it into. Although so

called canvas frames exist, they are limited in variety and availability, so many framers end up using regular frames for stretched canvas. The trick is holding the canvas in. Generally, framing components are secured in the frame by inserting a point or brad into the side of the frame recess, but if you can't get at the recess, this is impossible. There are three methods that exist to get you around this problem.

OPTION ONE: Canvas clips are brackets that fit over the backs of stretcher bars and wedge into the space between the stretcher bar and frame recess, securing them (Figure X-1). **OPTION TWO:** Offset clips have two right-angle bends forming off-setting flat ends between a vertical upright. One of the flat ends is screwed into the back of the frame while the other end overlaps the stretcher bar, holding it in (Figure X-2). Op-

Figure X-1: Canvas clips wedge into the space between the stretcher bar and the rabbet.

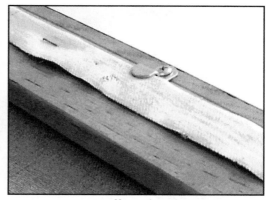

Figure X-2: Offset clips have two right angle bends forming off-setting flat ends between a vertical upright.

Figure X-3: A screweye set into the back of the frame provides a loop through which a regular screw can be inserted.

tion Three: A screweye set into the back of the frame provides a loop through which a regular screw can be inserted into the side of the stretcher bar, securing it (Figure X-3).

Mounting Needle Art

Needle art can be mounted quickly and easily with acid-free needlework tape. To better preserve needle art and keep it out of contact with adhesive, you may want to mount it by pinning and lacing. Cut a sheet of 3/16" thick foamboard about 3 inches smaller on each dimension than your canvas. Arrange some cotton batting in the middle of the foamboard and then place your canvas face up on top of it. Stretch your canvas around the edges of the foamboard uniformly at each edge and insert straight pins through the

canvas into the soft core of the foamboard (Figure X-4). After pinning, many framers also lace the needlework across the back of the foamboard in a crisscross fashion.

Mounting 3-Dimensional Objects

For the greatest flexibility in mounting three-dimensional objects, your mounting surface should be foamboard. You will, of course, want to cover it with an attractive fabric like velvet or felt, but you will need the soft, workable nature of foamboard to employ the widest range of mounting methods. To mount loose items like necklaces, handkerchiefs and scarves, sew them to the surface of the mounting board using invisible thread and a pilot needle. For sports jerseys and other apparel, insert a sheet of cardboard or matboard into the item to give it form and stability, then sew through the item and into the foamboard. For balls and other round objects, make a shallow crater in the surface of the foamboard, cut away a small circle in the fabric over the crater, apply a dollop of silicone rubber sealant and press the object in place. For cups, jars and other open-mouthed objects, cut a hole in the foamboard, slit the fabric over the hole and imbed the object in the surface. For knives, guns, spoons and plates, there are acrylic fixtures called Mighty Mounts that are designed to be anchored into foamboard to hold such objects. Mighty Mounts can be used for a wide range of other objects you may wish to mount.

Figure X-4: Stretch your canvas around the edges of the foamboard and insert straight pins into the core along each edge.

CHAPTER SEVEN

Glazing, Fitting and Finishing Your Frame

After you have mounted your artwork, you are ready for the final stages of your framing project.

Glazing Your Artwork

"Glazing" is the framer's way of saying that you're putting glass over the artwork; and it would suffice to say just that except that sometimes you don't use glass, you use acrylic. Acrylic, the clear, unbreakable plastic often referred to by the brand name Plexiglas, has several advantages over glass that make it desirable in certain circumstances.

The primary advantage of acrylic is how lightweight it is. When your frame is larger than 24"x 36", it's wise to opt for acrylic. The difference in weight is remarkable and glass is dangerous to handle in such large sizes. Acrylic

has the added advantage of being virtually unbreakable; so if you need to ship your artwork, acrylic is the better choice. On the other hand, acrylic scratches easily and must be cleaned with a soft cloth and plastic cleaner. Moreover, acrylic carries a high static charge and is risky to use with loose media like pastels and charcoals.

Acrylic usually comes covered with a protective mask. If you are reducing acrylic to size from a larger sheet, you can size it with the protective mask on, but when you are ready to clean it, peel away the mask from both sides (Figure Y-1). As the mask comes off, it will cling to the surface, betraying the static charge. Choose a plastic cleaner that has an anti-static agent (Figure Y-2) and then take it a step further by investing in an anti-static brush.

To clean acrylic, spray one side and wipe it down with a soft cloth. Avoid using paper towels as they can cause light surface abrasions in acrylic. As long as your plastic cleaner contains an anti-static agent, you can wipe the surface dry before turning it over to clean the other side. After cleaning both sides, use the anti-static brush to further reduce the static

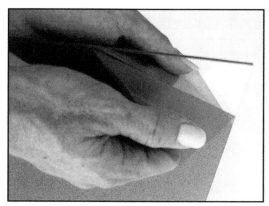

Figure Y-1: Peel the protective mask away from the acrylic.

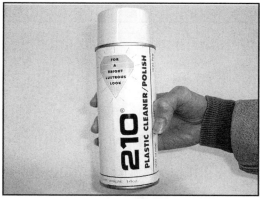

Figure Y-2: Use a plastic cleaner with an anti-static agent.

charge (Figure Y-3).

When cleaning glass, apply glass cleaner liberally to one side and then wait a few moments, letting the solvents in the cleaner break down dirt

Figure Y-3: Use an anti-static brush to further reduce static.

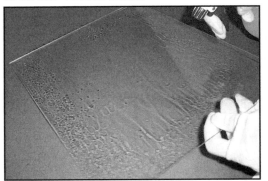

Figure Y-4: Leave the glass wet for a moment, letting the solvents break down dirt and oils.

and oils (Figure Y-4). Wipe the glass, but avoid wiping it completely dry. Leave it moist and let it air dry the rest of the way. The action of wiping a paper towel across the dry surface of glass increases static charge and is one reason why dust and lint suddenly reappear inside the glass after you've carefully inspected it to be sure it's free of such nuisances. The other reason for the sudden appearance of dust and lint is the bellows effect created when you press down on the framing components as they are loaded into the frame (Figure Y-5). Pressing down and releasing the components creates a suction that draws dust, lint and paper scraps into the air space between the glazing and the artwork. To prevent this, seal the edges of the stack of framing components with white artist's tape or acid-free masking tape before loading them into the frame (Figure Y-6).

Loading and Securing Your Framing Components

You now have everything you need to load the frame. If you have not already done so, stack your framing components together. If your artwork is mounted to foamboard, you won't need anything else behind it. On the other hand, if your artwork is mounted to a mat blank, you will want foamboard behind it to provide stability and fill the frame. Place your glazing over your matted, backed artwork, turn the stack over and place it in the frame (Figure Z-1).

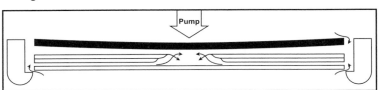

Figure Y-5: When you press down on the stack of contents, it creates a bellows effect, suctioning in dust and debris.

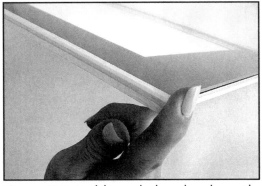

Figure Y-6: Seal the stack along the edges with white artist's tape or acid-free masking tape.

Figure Z-1: Place the stack in the frame.

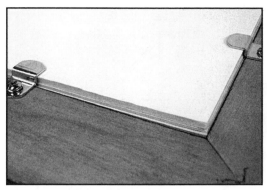

Figure Z-2: If the stack is too thick for the rabbet, use offset clips to hold it in.

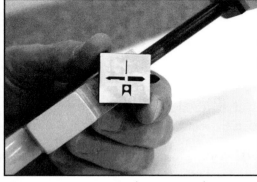

Figure Z-3: Rotate the turret to the setting for the point or brad of your choice.

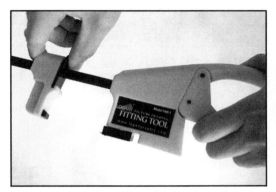

Figure Z-4: Press the release tab to slide the foot away from the body.

Figure Z-5: Insert a point or brad into the turret, making sure the pointed end is sticking out.

In most cases the stack of components will drop down, allowing you access to the interior wall of the rabbet. This is where you will drive a point or brad to secure the contents of the frame. From time to time, however, the stack may be too thick, preventing access to the rabbet. If this happens, use offset clips to secure the contents. Offset clips are equipped with two right-angle bends forming off-setting flat ends between a vertical upright. One of the flat ends is screwed into the back of the frame while the other end overlaps the stack, holding it in (Figure Z-2).

Logan Frame Fitting Tool

When the stack sits low enough in the frame to allow access to the rabbet, you will be able to use the Logan Fitting Tool Model 400-1. The process of loading and securing the contents in the frame is called "fitting"

the frame. Thus, the name of this product. The Logan Fitting Tool is a unique device that inserts a variety of different points and brads, eliminating the need to own different devices to insert different points. The operation is simple.

STEP ONE: Choose the type of point or brad you want to use. The Fitting Tool can take framer's points, flexi-points, multi-points or brads. Rotate the turret to the setting for the point or brad of your choice (Figure Z-3).

STEP TWO: Press the release tab and slide the foot away from the body (Figure Z-4).

STEP THREE: Insert a point or brad into the turret, making sure the pointed end is sticking out (Figure Z-5).

STEP FOUR: Rest the body of the device on the back of the framing components. Move the body forward until the tip of the point is pressing against the interior wall of the frame rabbet (Figure Z-6).

STEP FIVE: Slide the foot back until it contacts the outside of the frame (Figure Z-7).

STEP SIX: Firmly squeeze the handle, driving the point into the interior wall of the frame rabbet (Figure Z-8). Caution: For best results keep the base of the device flat against the back of the framing components.

STEP SEVEN: Press the release tab and slide the foot away from the frame (Figure Z-9). As a general rule points or

brads should be spaced about every 4" to 5" (Figure Z-10). Insert your first point about 2" in from a corner. Repeat for the remaining points.

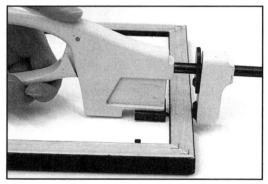

Figure Z-6: Move the body forward until the tip of the tab is resting against the inside of the rabbet.

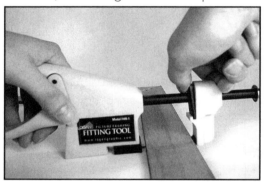

Figure Z-7: Slide the foot back until it contacts the outside of the frame.

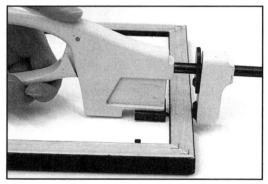

Figure Z-8: Firmly squeeze the handle, driving the point into the rabbet.

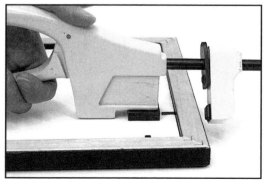

Figure Z-9: Press the release tab and slide the foot away from the frame.

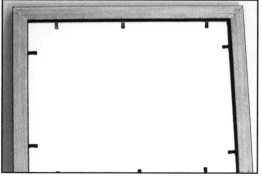

Figure Z-10: Points should be placed every 4" to 5".

Logan Dual Drive Elite Point Driver

For greater versatility in driving points into different types of frames, and for increased speed and accuracy, you may prefer the Dual Drive Elite Point Driver. This tool drives points with authority into hardwood and softwood frames. Spring-loaded and trigger-driven, it fires points from a stacked magazine, securing the contents in mere seconds.

STEP ONE: To load the Dual Drive Elite Point Driver, thumb back the release button on top of the device and slide back the point loading cover (Figure Z-11).

STEP TWO: Install the points which are stacked magazine-style in a strip. Place the strip in the magazine slot and close the point loading cover (Figure Z-12).

STEP THREE: Adjust the knob at the back of the device to increase or decrease the drive strength for penetrating hardwoods or softwoods (Figure Z-13).

STEP FOUR: Place the nose of the point driver against the inside of the frame rabbet (Figure Z-14). Keep the bottom of it flat on the frame contents. Don't lift or angle the driver.

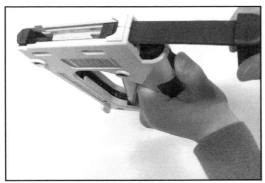

Figure Z-11: Slide back the point loading cover.

Figure Z-12: The strip of points in the magazine slot.

Figure Z-13: Adjust the drive strength.

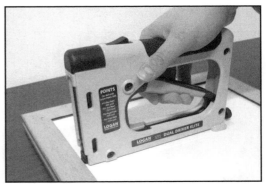

Figure Z-14: Place the nose of the driver against the inside of the frame rabbet.

STEP FIVE: Squeeze the trigger to drive the point (Figure Z-15).

STEP SIX: Repeat, spacing the points about 5″ apart, and about 2″ in from the corners.

When you are finished securing the con-

Figure Z-15: Squeeze the trigger to drive the point.

Figure AA-1: Cut the paper so that it's larger than the frame.

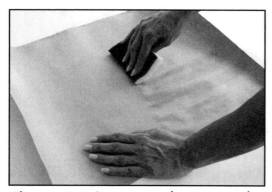

Figure AA-2: Dampen the paper with a wet cloth or sponge.

tents in the frame, you are ready to install the dust cover.

Installing a Dust Cover

The dust cover is the paper that covers and seals the back of the frame. In addition to preventing dust and insects from getting into the interior space it conceals the inner workings from clients and provides a nice finishing touch. This is where many frame shops put their promotional stickers.

Installing a dust cover is entirely optional. If you are framing for yourself and don't foresee dust or insects as a major problem, you might want to skip this step, especially if you've already sealed the edges of the stack of framing components with tape. If you do choose to install a dust cover, the process is fairly simple and made easier with the right tools and helpful insights.

STEP ONE: Cut your paper. Two types of paper are widely used for dust covers, either brown Kraft paper, also known as mailing paper, or acid-free frame backing paper. The latter is preferred for archival frame jobs. Cut the paper so it is about an inch wider on each edge than the frame size (Figure AA-1).

STEP TWO: Dampen the paper with a wet cloth or sponge (Figure AA-2).

STEP THREE: Squeeze a bead of white glue onto the back of the frame (Figure AA-3).

Figure AA-3: Squeeze a bead of white glue onto the back of the frame.

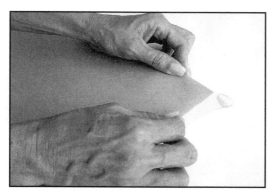

Figure AA-4: Crease the edges of the paper to the edges of the frame.

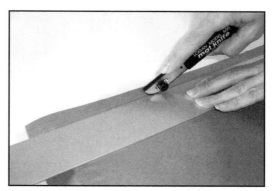

Figure AA-5: Use a straightedge and mat knife to trim the paper to the edge of the frame.

Spread it out thin with a wadded paper towel.

STEP FOUR: Place the dampened paper on the back of the frame. Wait one hour for the paper to dry. To hasten things, use a blow dryer. As the paper dries, it will shrink, pulling as tight as a drum.

STEP FIVE: Crease the edges of the paper to the edges of the frame (Figure AA-4).

STEP SIX: Use a straightedge and mat knife to trim the paper to the edge of the frame (Figure AA-5).

Installing Hanging Hardware

Several options exist for hanging your artwork but the preferred method is picture hanging wire because it provides the greatest ease and flexibility with artwork of any size. Traditionally screweyes have been used for attaching hanging wire to the frame but in recent years strap hangers with D rings have grown in popularity because they lie flat against the back of the dust cover and won't scratch the wall.

To position screweyes or strap hangers, measure about one-third down from the top of the frame and mark the location. You don't have to be exact in your placement of the hanging hardware. If the two hangers are not exactly aligned with each other, the artwork may not hang straight. But then, of course, you will shift the wire on the nail until it does hang straight.

To attach a screweye to soft or medium wood frames, make a pilot hole in the back of the frame with a scratch awl (Figure BB-1). Start turning the screweye by hand until it becomes too resistant (Figure BB-2). Then use

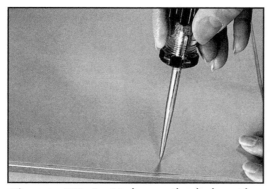

Figure BB-1: Make a pilot hole with a scratch awl.

Figure BB-2: Start turning the screw by hand.

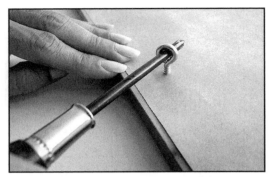

Figure BB-3: Use the barrel of a screwdriver to turn the screw the rest of the way.

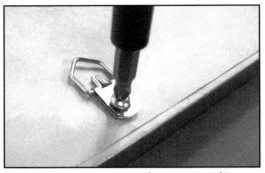

Figure BB-4: Attach a strap hanger with a screwdriver.

the barrel of the screwdriver or a screweye twirler to turn the screweye the rest of the way (Figure BB-3). To attach a screweye to hardwood frames, pre-drill a hole with a power drill.

To attach a strap hanger to soft or medium wood frames, make a pilot hole in the back of the frame with a scratch awl. Turn the screw into the wood with a screwdriver (Figure BB-4). To attach a strap hanger into hardwood frames, pre-drill a hole with a power drill and attach the screw with a power screwdriver.

Installing Hanging Wire and Bumper Pads

Traditional braided picture wire provides the necessary strength for hanging but tends to fray at the ends, jabbing the user. Wire with a plastic coating effectively keeps the wire from unbraiding while allowing the wire to retain its pliability. Hanging wire typically comes in three strengths: 19 lb., 25 lb. and 43

lb. Each strength is a measure of the weight-bearing capacity of the wire. If the framed piece is too heavy for the wire, the wire will unravel, pulling free of the hangers, regardless of the complexity of the knots used. If the wire is adequate to hold the weight, it adds nothing to the wire's holding power to tie a complex knot. For this reason, the wire should be secured simply by coiling it around itself.

To attach the wire, insert one end through the D ring of your strap hanger (Figure CC-1) and coil it around itself several times. Stretch the wire across to the other hanger and pull it taut. Don't worry about leaving any slack in the wire. In spite of your best efforts at pulling it taut, you will end up with some slack, and there is no harm in leaving the wire relatively taut. It just means your framed piece will hang tight against the wall, which is desirable anyway. Allow for about 3-5 inches of wire to feed through the D ring on the opposite side. Clip off the excess wire (Figure CC-2) and

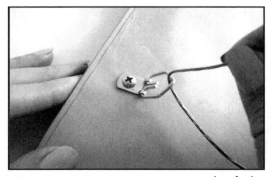

Figure CC-1: Insert one end of the hanging wire through the hanger.

Figure CC-2: Clip off the excess with wire cutters.

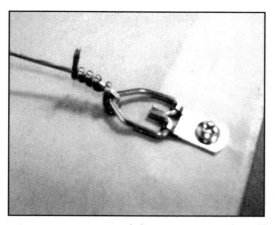

Figure CC-3: Coil the wire around itself several times.

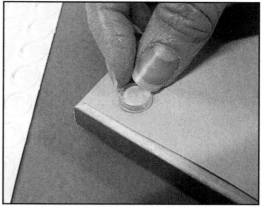

Figure CC-4: Adhere bumper pads to each corner.

coil the remaining wire around itself several times (Figure CC-3).

For a nice finishing touch, attach self-adhesive bumper pads to each corner on the back of your frame. These will prevent the frame from scratching the wall. The pads simply peel off a sheet of release paper and adhere to the dust cover (Figure CC-4).

Attaching the bumper pads is the final step in the process. Your matted, mounted, glazed and framed artwork is now ready to hang.

Conclusion

By being able to do your own framing, you've arrived at a place where the gratification of a job well done intersects with the satisfaction of having saved time and money. This is a place where, until recently, non-professionals were virtually excluded. But now, with the advent of inexpensive and reliable framing tools, anyone can frame for themselves at home or in a small business. For a modest investment you can cut mats, build wooden frames, mount artwork and perform quality framing for as much as 75 percent less than it would cost to have it done by a professional.

On the other hand, if you still want to avail yourself of the expertise provided by a professional, that option still exists. Only now it's not the only option. Now there are other ways to frame, and that's how it should be—a choice for any budget, the flexibility to welcome all who aspire, a situation that bodes well for the future of picture framing as art and aptitude.

For more information visit **LoganGraphic.com**

Art Courtesy of D.M. Moore

Framing Tools and Accessories

LOGAN®
GRAPHIC PRODUCTS, INC.
Tools for Art - Tools for Life

Logan F200-2
Precision Sander Elite
- Sand miters to perfect 45° angles
- Accepts up to 3-1/2" (8 cm) width moulding
- Includes free set up and operation DVD

Logan F300-1
Studio Joiner
- Joins frames with moulding up to 2-1/2" (6 cm) in width
- Uses hard or soft v-nails
- Includes free set up and operation DVD

Logan F300-2
Pro Joiner
- Joins frames with moulding up to 2-1/2" (6 cm) in width
- Can drive two v-nails at a time using adjustable nail blocks
- Includes free set up and operation DVD

POINT DRIVING TOOLS

Logan F400-1
Fitting Tool
- Drives rigid or flexible points plus multi-points and brad nails
- Drives single points one at a time in up to 2-1/2" (6 cm) width moulding

Logan F500-2
Dual Drive Elite
- Drives rigid or flexible points strips
- Adjustable tension for hard or soft woods
- Uses point strips for repeat point firing

Handheld Mat Cutters

LOGAN®
GRAPHIC PRODUCTS, INC.
Tools for Art - Tools for Life

Logan 1100
Freestyle Bevel Cutter
• Cut freestyle designs into matboard
• Easy to use with either left or right hand

Logan 2000
Push Style Bevel Cutter
• Retractable blade
• Start-and-stop indicator

Logan 4000
Deluxe Pull Style Bevel Cutter
• Pivot and pull blade action
• Start and stop indicator
• Ergonomic blade holder for comfortable operation
• Includes marker bar

Logan 5000
8-Ply Bevel Cutter
• Cuts both 4-ply and 8-ply matboard
• Depth indicator light tells you when the blade is properly inserted
• Can be used on any Logan equipment with cutting heads that hook on

Specialty Accessories

Logan 201
Oval & Circle Cutter
• Fast, portable, easy to use
• No other equipment required

Logan 703
Artists V-Groover
• No trimming or taping required to produce v-grooves
• Works with Compact series and 401, 450, 450-1, 550-1, 560-1, 750, 760, 750-1, 760-1 series Logan Mat Cutters

Logan 705
Logan V-Groover
• No trimming or taping required to produce v-grooves
• Works with 600, 650, 655, 660 Logan Mat Cutters

Logan 706
Universal V-Groover
• No trimming or taping required to produce v-grooves
• Works with Logan Platinum Edge or mat cutters using a 5/8" wide cutting bar rod

Board Mounted Mat Cutters

LOGAN®
GRAPHIC PRODUCTS, INC.
Tools for Art - Tools for Life

Logan 250
Craft & Hobby Cutter
- 23" (58 cm) capacity
- Includes push style bevel cutting head & mat knife
- Lightweight, portable, easy to transport
- Includes free set up and operation DVD

Logan 301-1
Compact Classic Mat Cutter
- 32" (81 cm) capacity base board with guide rail and mat guide
- Includes push style bevel cutter & mat knife
- Includes free set up and operation DVD

Logan 350-1
Compact Elite Mat Cutter
- 32" (81 cm) capacity base board with guide rail, mat guide, measuring bar and production stops
- Includes push style bevel cutter and straight cutting head
- Includes free set up and operation DVD

Logan 450-1
Artists Elite Mat Cutter
- 40" (101 cm) capacity base board with guide rail, mat guide, measuring bar and production stops
- Includes pull style bevel cutter & straight cutter
- Includes free set up and operation DVD

Logan 550-1
Simplex Classic Mat Cutter
- 40" (101 cm) capacity base board with guide rail, mat guide, 27" scaled squaring arm and production stops
- Includes pull style bevel cutting head and straight cutting head
- Also available in 60" (152 cm) capacity as model 560-1
- Includes free set up and operation DVD

Logan 750-1
Simplex Elite Mat Cutter
- 40" (101 cm) capacity base board with guide rail, mat guide, 27" scaled squaring arm and production stops
- Includes pull style bevel cutting head and straight cutting head
- Also includes glass cutter, 8-Ply bevel cutter, acrylic plastic cutter, paper trimmer accessories plus a copy of the Home Picture Framing Book
- Also available in 60" (152 cm) capacity as model 760-1
- Includes free set up and operation DVD

Logan 650-1
Framer's Edge
- 40" (101 cm) capacity base board with guide rail, mat guide, 27" scaled squaring arm and movable production stops
- Includes a dual purpose bevel and straight cutting head with start and stop indicator
- Also available in a 48" (121 cm) capacity as model 655 & as 60" (152 cm) capacity as model 660
- Includes free set up and operation DVD

Straight Edges

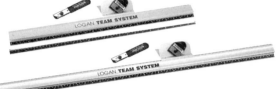

Logan 524, 540 & 560
Adapt-A-Rule
- Scaled straight edges with rubber strip underside to preventing slipping.
- Used to guide various Logan cutting heads for more accurate cuts.
- Works with push or pull style cutting heads that hook on.
- Available in three sizes
  #524 24" (61 cm)
  #540 40" (101 cm)
  #560 60" (152 cm) - no scale or rubber stripping on model 560

Logan 424-1 & 440-1
Team System Plus
- Complete mat cutting system including either a 24" (61 cm) or 40" (101 cm) scaled straight edge with rubberized bottom plus push style bevel cutting head and 500 Logan mat knife.
- Available in two sizes
  #424-1 24" (61 cm)
  #440-1 40" (101 cm)

Accessories

Logan 701-1
Straight Cutter Elite
- Pull-type 90° cutter with ergonomic handle
- Three depth settings including storage, standard 4-ply matboard and 3/16 (.05 cm) foam board
- Can be used on any Logan equipment with cutting heads that hook on

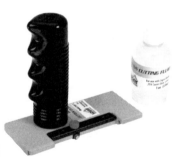

Logan 704-1
Glass Cutter Elite
- Pull-type glass cutter with hardened steel wheel
- Includes cutting fluid
- Sizes glass used for general framing

Logan 500
Mat Knife
- Sizes matboard at a 90° angle
- Three depth settings including storage, standard 4-ply matboard and 3/16 (.05 cm) foam board

Logan 1500
Foam Board Cutter
- Push style 90 or 45 degree foam board cutter
- Cuts up to 3/8" thick foam board